GCSE
Success

Computer Science

Revision Guide

Sharon Angland

Fundamentals of Algorithms

Programming 1

Programming 2

Programming 3

Contents

Fundamentals of Data Representation

Computer Systems

Fundamentals of Computer Networks

Cyber Security and Ethics

Algorithms

An algorithm is a process used to solve a problem or achieve a task. In computer science, sometimes a program is used. Be careful not to confuse the two! A program is a type of algorithm, but then so is a recipe.

An algorithm:

➤ is a set of steps, or instructions, to complete a task. We use them all the time – we just don't realise we are.

➤ is a way to solve problems, or complete tasks. There are a lot of different ways in which to complete each task, just like there are a lot of different Victoria sponge cake recipes or there is more than one way to go to school.

➤ is judged by whether it completes the task, or solves the problem, in the **most efficient way**. An efficient algorithm only uses the resources it absolutely needs in order to complete the task – no more, no less

➤ is generally made up of INPUT – PROCESS – OUTPUT.

➤ is tracked using what are called **trace tables**, which trace the progress of the computer through the code.

Algorithms help us tackle a range of problems, not just computer coding.

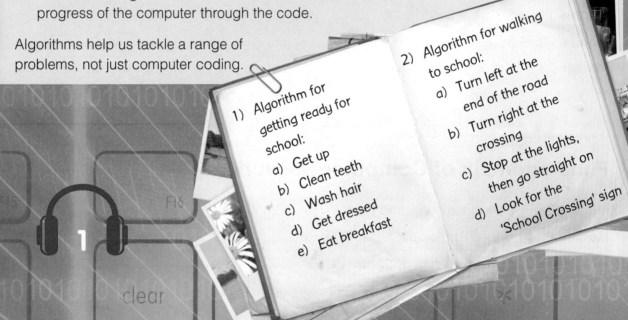

1) Algorithm for getting ready for school:
a) Get up
b) Clean teeth
c) Wash hair
d) Get dressed
e) Eat breakfast

2) Algorithm for walking to school:
a) Turn left at the end of the road
b) Turn right at the crossing
c) Stop at the lights, then go straight on
d) Look for the 'School Crossing' sign

Process and function

Algorithms are generally made up of INPUT – PROCESS – OUTPUT. Keeping track of what the code is doing at any one time can be challenging, so we use trace tables, which trace the progress of the computer through the code.

INPUT ➡ PROCESS ➡ OUTPUT

When you use a trace table, you go through your code as if you are the computer, writing down the inputs, the processes and the outputs. This is an essential part of testing and can help you see where the computer code would go wrong before you even enter it, which saves time in class – and money in business.

KEYWORDS

Efficiency ➤ The extent to which a task is completed in the shortest possible amount of code. This also relates to the amount of memory used and speed of execution of the code.

Trace tables ➤ A template to help you follow each instruction in your program

Flowcharts

Flowcharts are a great visual way to plan a program through a sequence of events.

Simple Burglar Alarm Set:

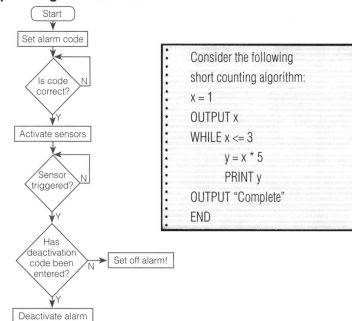

Trace tables

A trace table allows you to work through an algorithm or program to iron out any potential problems.

Consider the following short counting algorithm:

```
x = 1
OUTPUT x
WHILE x <= 3
    y = x * 5
    PRINT y
OUTPUT "Complete"
END
```

Line	x	y	Output
1	1		
2			1
3			
4		5	
5			5
3	2		
4		10	
5			10
3	3		
4		15	
5			15
6			Complete

Decomposition

When you decompose a task, you break it into smaller tasks.

Decomposition:

➤ helps you write your code because it is usually easier to write code for each section at a time, rather than trying to write the whole thing in one go. So, an alarm system for your home will have a 'set/unset' program and a 'live' program.

➤ makes life a lot easier when you are testing your code because you can test each section before you run it all together. Think about the code needed to run a driverless car – you can see why it is a good idea to test the bits of code (like stopping when something is in the way) before you put the car on the road.

TIDYING MY ROOM
1) Clear the floor
2) Move what's under the bed
3) Put clothes in the drawer

Abstraction

Abstraction is the way we remove unneeded information from a task so a computer can complete it. In the exam, you will need to be able to read code, or a brief, and identify the 'real problem'. For example, if you are programming a driverless car, does it matter if the car is pink or yellow? What is more important is whether speed or direction is set accurately.

 Make a model of a computer showing INPUT – PROCESS – OUTPUT, or be more ambitious and include storage! Show how data travels through the system.

1. What is an algorithm? Explain using **two** different examples: one in human terms, and one referring to computers.
2. What do we mean by an 'efficient algorithm'?
3. What are the main components of algorithms?
4. How does a trace table help with efficient code design?

Searching

Searching is a basic and common task for an algorithm. For example, your phone searches for a signal and your computer looks for an internet link. There are **two** main types of search algorithm that you need to know: **binary** and **linear**.

Binary search

A binary search chooses the middle value in a sorted **array**, and works out whether the value sought is higher or lower than the middle value. Then it splits the array again to check again – is the value higher or lower than the middle value? The list is repeatedly split in half and half and half until the item is located.

This means that the computer only ever searches half of the data, because it is either on the correct number, or pointed at the correct half of the data that is in the array.

We use this method in our own lives, too. If you're looking for a student in a class whose surname begins with H, you would not start at A.

In pseudocode, the binary search algorithm is short. Follow the code through step by step:

```
ClassList= [5,6,8,9,15]          ←  The content of the array is
INPUT A #number you're looking for   inside the [] brackets.
IF (first > last) return –1; # number not found represented by –1
ELSE                             # identifies a comment
{                                  ignored by the computer.

    INT mid = (first + last)/2;      == means "is equal to".
    IF (value = = A[mid])
        RETURN mid;
    ELSE IF (value < A[mid])
        BinarySearch(A, first, mid-1, value);
    ELSE
        BinarySearch(A, mid+1, last, value);
}  ←                             The program is contained
END                                within the {} brackets.
```

Another example of this is shown below:

A group of students have received their test results. To find out which student got 9, the computer would first sort these students and their grades in the left column into grade order in the right column:

Alex: 5   Alex: 5
Bailey: 9   Riley: 6
Chris: 8   Chris: 8
Jamie: 15   Bailey: 9
Riley: 6   Jamie: 15

In a binary search, the computer would start in the middle, with Chris, at 8 marks. That's too low, so it would split the top half in two, which would leave the middle entry at Bailey, who gained 9 marks.

KEYWORDS

Array ➤ A set of data items of the same type grouped together using one identifying label or identifier

Linear search

A linear search:

➤ is used when you can't sort the data into any useful order, or when there are very few items to search.
➤ is also known as 'brute force' searching. The computer searches from the first item until either the end of the data or until the item sought is located, one by one.
➤ is best used when the data to be searched is very small, or is so frequently amended that sorting is a waste of time.
➤ can take a really, really long time because it checks every single item, which is why it is used only when a binary search isn't possible or appropriate.

The pseudocode for this type of search is much more straightforward. Follow it through in the graphic below.

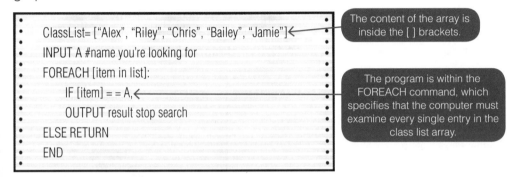

```
ClassList= ["Alex", "Riley", "Chris", "Bailey", "Jamie"]
INPUT A #name you're looking for
FOREACH [item in list]:
    IF [item] = = A,
    OUTPUT result stop search
ELSE RETURN
END
```

The content of the array is inside the [ ] brackets.

The program is within the FOREACH command, which specifies that the computer must examine every single entry in the class list array.

Binary vs linear

When selecting the most suitable search algorithm, consider these summary points:

➤ Data must be already sorted before a binary search can be carried out.
➤ A linear search can be slower as it checks every piece of data.
➤ With very small data sets neither method would have a particular speed advantage.
➤ A linear search can be completed with a shorter pseudocode sequence.

In pairs: use a suit of playing cards – so just the spades or hearts for example – and while one of you thinks of a card in the suit, the other one uses binary search to locate it. Compare that with wild guessing to see the effectiveness of a systematic search.

1. Imagine you are looking for a telephone number for K. Lombard in London, which of the two search techniques would be the best? Explain your answer.
2. Show how you would use binary search to find the person with 17 marks from this group: 22, 19, 17, 15, 2, 9.
3. Which search technique requires data to be sorted?

Sorting

An important part of managing data, sorting algorithms allows us to find things quickly by putting data into some sort of order. This might be putting names into alphabetical order or finding the cheapest online console game.

Merge sort

Merge sort is also known as 'divide and conquer' because, like the binary search, the merge sort splits the data in half and works on each half in turn. The computer then sorts the smaller groups before merging the two together again. This is rather like when we shuffle cards, only we mess up the sort while the computer code resets it.

To complete a merge sort, the computer follows two steps.
1. It repeatedly splits the data into two halves until each 'list' contains only a single data item.
2. Having broken it into smaller parts, it repeatedly merges these 'lists' back together, this time putting them in their required order (ascending or **descending** in value).

```
MergeSort (Array(First..Last))
BEGIN
IF Array contains only one element THEN
        RETURN Array #already sorted
ELSE
        Middle= ((Last + First)/2) #rounded down to the nearest integer
        LeftSide = MergeSort(Array(First..Middle))
        RightSide = MergeSort(Array(Middle+1..Last))
    Result = Merge(LeftSide, RightSide)
    RETURN Result
    ENDIF
    END MergeSort
```

Bubble sort

Bubble sort comes from the way that stones settle in a tank of bubbling water: the larger stones sink to the bottom of the tank while the small ones appear to rise to the top. That is why a bubble sort is called a sinking sort. This is very rarely used, but it illustrates important principles so is included in all computer science study. Its slow methodical nature means it is normally only used for very small volumes of data.

➤ A bubble sort compares the first two items, checks which one is larger, and swaps them if necessary so that the larger is first.

➤ Then it checks the next pair, and so on.

➤ If there have been any position changes, the whole process is begun again until the computer can go from start to finish and there are no changes to be made. At this point the data is in descending order.

KEYWORDS

Descending ➤ Decreasing in number to 1 downwards, or in value from A

 Sorting algorithms

Module 3

3

A practical example of this is worked through below.

I have a list of grades [5,6,8,9,15] and need to sort them from highest to lowest.
The computer looks at the first two: [5,6]
The second (right hand) is larger, so they are swapped [6,5]. Then the next two are checked [5,8].
Again, these need to be swapped [8,5].
The next two are [5,9] which, again, have to be changed (see how the 5 is being pushed down to the bottom) [9,5]
Finally [5,15] have to be swapped to [15,5].

In one pass, the list has been changed from [5,6,8,9,15] to [6,8,9,15,5]. The computer will have to do this sequence again, from the start, to change the list and slowly, pass by pass, move this to [15,9,8,6,5]. The numbers would change like this, in ELEVEN steps:

[5,6,8,9,15]   [8,9,15,6,5]
[6,5,8,9,15]   [9,8,15,6,5]
[6,8,5,9,15]   [9,15,8,6,5]
[6,8,9,5,15]   [15,9,8,6,5]
[6,8,9,15,5]
[8,6,9,15,5]
[8,9,6,15,5]

Values that are already in the 'right place' don't move again.

The code for this is a lot shorter:

```
FOR i from 1 to N

    FOR j from 0 to N - 1

        IF a[j] > a[j + 1]

            SWAP (a[j], a[j + 1])
```

For the exam, you need to be able to compare and contrast these two types of sorting algorithms.

	Bubble	Merge
Efficiently handle big data sets?	No	Yes
Speed	Usually slower	Faster
Space used in memory	Stable (never changes since items are just swapped)	Variable (splits the data in two)

In a box, mix up small and large stones or marbles. If you shake them (gently) you will see bubble sort in process, as the larger stones or marbles come to the top.

1. You need to work out the oldest person in a class of 20. Which would be the most appropriate of the two sort techniques? Explain your answer.
2. Show how you would use bubble sort to create a descending list from this group: 22, 19, 17, 15, 2, 9.
3. Which sort technique is appropriate for large amounts of data?

Fundamentals of algorithms

Definitions

Decomposition → Break tasks into smaller bits

Abstraction → Cut out the unimportant stuff

Array → Arrangement of data in computer memory

Single dimension → Like a list: just one sequence of items

Multi dimension → Like a table or grade book: more than one sequence of items

INPUT – PROCESS – OUTPUT → Basic elements of any algorithm

Algorithm → Process to solve problems

Tools

Minimum memory

Trace tables

Check efficiency → Shortest code

Check efficiency → Resources allocated

Comments in the code → Help programmer see what does what

Help in testing one part at a time

Search and sort

Search → Binary → Start in the middle and work up or down

Search → Linear → Brute force: start at the beginning and go on to the end or until data located

Sort → Bubble → Compare pairs and swap where needed

Sort → Merge → Split in two, sort the two, then put back together

Answer the following questions on a separate piece of paper.

1. Complete the trace table for the algorithm below.

```
number = 5
OUTPUT number
FOR i from 1 to 3
    number = number +3
    OUTPUT number
END
```

Line	Number	i	Output
1	5		
2			5
3		1	
4			
5			
6			
3			
4			
5			
3			
4			
5			

(8 marks)

2. Decompose the task: an automatic car wash program that will wash all vehicles from a small car to a minibus. **(5 marks)**

3. Decompose the task: make your bedroom neat enough for an inspection. **(2 marks)**

4. Explain how decomposition helps programmers code efficiently. **(3 marks)**

5. Explain how abstraction helps programmers to plan a coding solution to a problem. **(3 marks)**

6. Describe what this algorithm does.

```
counter = 1
WHILE counter < 11
    PRINT counter
    counter = counter + 1
PRINT "All done"
END
```

(2 marks)

7. Explain how the efficiency of algorithms is judged. **(3 marks)**

8. Compare and contrast linear and binary search algorithms. **(5 marks)**

9. Compare and contrast merge sort and bubble sort algorithms. **(3 marks)**

Main data types

Data types allow us to categorise the range of data that is used in programs. Computer programs treat different types of data in different ways.

Here are the main data types:

Integer is a whole number, no decimal point or fraction, no letters. It might be used to define a count for a loop – you can only perform an instruction a whole number of times, not 2½ times, for example. (It's a term you might have met in maths.)

Boolean data is digital: yes/no; on/off; true/false. This is essential for loops – for example, is the temperature over a set point? Has the loop been run x number of times? (You should have met this as part of your work learning how to search the Internet effectively.)

Real data tries to reflect 'real' numbers, so this includes decimals: these are sometimes described as 'float' numbers because the number of decimal places can vary depending on the level of detail needed. It might be used to show the weight of an item in kilos, or fractions of distance measurement. Being specific about 4.75 kilos, not 5, for example, could make a difference for dosage of medication or fertiliser.

Character is any one of the letters and symbols on a keyboard. You can also define a number as a character when you don't want to use it for a mathematical operation.

String can hold any number of alphanumeric characters: text, number, symbol. This can include name, address and telephone number entries, for example. Although a telephone number is constructed of numbers, we don't use it for mathematical operations: it is effectively an address, so it is stored as a string.

Data Type	Example Use
Integer	loopCount = int(a/b)
Boolean	heatingOn = true
Real	weightInKilos = 2.742
Character	Sex = "F"
String	PhoneNumber = "012115489721"

Programming concepts

There are three main constructs within coding: **sequence**, **iteration** (or **repetition**) and **selection** (or **choice**).

Constructs

Sequence is the simplest form, or structure, of computer code. The computer moves from one statement to the next in sequence. There are no loops, no branches, and no instructions can be skipped.

Sequence structure follows one path from start to finish.

Iteration (or **repetition**) refers to the number of times a computer passes through a set of instructions. One iteration is once through, and would be shown in a sequence-based code. We tend to use this term when referring to loops in code – for example, how many times (or iterations) will the computer complete this section of a code? There are two forms of iteration: **definite** (also called count control) sets the specific number of times an instruction must be performed and **indefinite** (also called condition control) allows for a variable number of times to perform the instruction, dependent on another factor, such as temperature, or weight or time.

Selection (or **choice**) is best demonstrated using the 'IF, THEN, ELSE' description. <u>If</u> the temperature is 14 degrees Celsius, <u>then</u> turn on the boiler, <u>else</u> leave the boiler off. Most computer code involves some element of selection.

Selection allows for a decision to change the flow of the program.

Module 4   Data types

Sequence	Iteration	Selection

Name <- USERINPUT
OUTPUT "Hi,"Name
OUTPUT "Press x to exit."
	FOR i ← 1 TO 10
	    OUTPUT i
	ENDFOR
		IF age < 15 THEN
		    age ← myVar + 1
		ELSE OUTPUT age
		ENDIF

Examples of codes that reflect the three main principles

Both iteration and selection can be used in **nested** forms, which mean that more than one loop or decision is 'inside' a larger part of the code.

In computer terms, the nested versions look neater than the longer sequences would:

NESTED ITERATION	NESTED SELECTION

WHILE Temp < 20
…Do Something
FOR I <- 1 TO 10
… Do Something else
ENDFOR
…More tasks
ENDWHILE
	IF Name="Fred" Then
	… Do Something
	IF LastName = "Flintstone"
	… Do Something else
	ENDIF
	… More tasks
	ENDIF

Other statement types

The main other statement types to know are: **variable declaration**, **constant declaration**, **assignment** and **subroutine** (also called **procedure** or **function**).
Variable declaration is when you allocate a memory space, a name and/or value to a variable. Variables by definition can change through the process of the program.
Constant declaration is when you allocate a name to a value. Usually this is then irrevocable: you cannot change the value or the name once declared without editing the code itself.
Assignment means assigning a value to a variable, such as Name="Fred". Commonly, the = sign is used for assignment of a value.

Names (or **identifiers**) are assigned to constants and variables to make it easier for the human programmer to read, create and follow the code. The computer doesn't change its response to the name of an allocation unless it is a key word for that programming language, but it makes sense to the programmer if the username entered is allocated to a variable called something like UserName.

What To Wear
Main Decision – is it a school day?
  a. Is it a 'non-uniform' day?
  b. Is the weather cold?
  c. Is the weather wet?
  d. Do I have games/PE/ science today?

Nested selection in human terms

Daily Operation
WHILE at School
    Go to location of school
    For Classes = 1 to 6
        Go to classes
    ENDFOR
    Go to any after-school clubs
ENDWHILE

Nested iteration in human terms

1. What is a Boolean data type?
2. Give an example of an integer.
3. What is iteration and how might use of iteration help a programmer writing code for a greenhouse temperature control system?

KEYWORDS

Definite ➤ Defined within the code, such as 'for 1= 1 to 5, do this'
Indefinite ➤ Variable and defined by another factor, such as 'while temperature above 20°C, hold the window open'
Nested ➤ When you put one element 'inside' another, such as 'putting on your blazer' is 'inside' 'getting ready for school'
Declaration ➤ When you 'declare' something you define it, such as 'AgeInDays = AGE × 365'
Identifier ➤ The way an element of the code (variable, constant or subroutine) is labelled

Data types | **Module 4** | 13

Using pseudocode

Pseudocode is the name we give to a shared language that coders understand and use for planning programs before beginning the coding. Computers cannot understand it, but it is not simple English either: it is a formalised way of writing that means coders from all over the world will be able to make sense of it.

In addition to established languages like Python or Java, all exam boards will have their own pseudocode 'dictionary' that will cover specifics that they expect. Make sure you have a copy of this dictionary – you'll need it for your revision.

If we used natural (or 'normal') English it would be too verbose – there would be too many words. Using one particular 'high level' language would make us too focused on the structure of that language rather than on a way to solve the task.

Characteristics of pseudocode

➤ Always starts with the name of the program
➤ Made up of a sequence of statements or steps
➤ Each statement is written on a separate line
➤ Statements are written in simple English
➤ Keywords and indentation are used to identify separate sections of the code
➤ No fixed syntax (so you don't have to worry about semi-colons or brackets)

Examples of pseudocode

1. Calculate the area of a rectangle.

Use CAPITAL letters to help with variable names.

```
INPUT HeightOfRectangle
INPUT WidthOfRectangle
AREA = HeightOfRectangle * WidthOfRectangle
DISPLAY AREA
END
```

2. Create code that identifies whether a student has passed or failed a test.

If a student scores 50 or more then they pass.

> You can show the instructions for the IF statement indented so this section is clear.

```
IF Score >= 50 THEN
        PRINT "Passed"
ELSE
        PRINT "Failed"
ENDIF
END
```

3. Calculate overtime for a set of workers.

> Brackets in code work the same as in maths lessons – operations in brackets are done first.

```
IF HoursWorked > NormalHours THEN
        Wage = (2 * (HoursWorked – NormalHours) +
        HoursWorked)* HourlyRate
ELSE
        Wage = HoursWorked * HourlyRate
ENDIF
END
```

Common commands in pseudocode

IF Something **THEN** do something else **ENDIF**
WHILE Something do something else **ENDWHILE**
FOR this is something incremented **TO** something else

KEYWORDS

Pseudocode ➤ The language used to construct programs in theory before using the appropriate computer language

Create flashcards to help you remember the commands and create large-scale pseudocode programs.

1. Write the pseudocode for making a cup of tea (or be ambitious and include the option for coffee!).
2. Explain the difference between pseudocode and 'natural' English.
3. What is the difference between IF and WHILE?

Arithmetic

One of the most common functions of computer code is **arithmetic**: **addition**, **subtraction**, **multiplication**, **division** (**real** and **integer**, with remainders).

Action	Symbol
Addition	+
Subtraction	–
Multiplication	*
Division	/
Exponent/Power	^

Division has two refining elements – MOD and DIV.

MOD (short for modulo or modulus), finds the remainder after a division calculation. 13 divided by 2, for example, is 6 remainder 1. The MOD operation would therefore return 1 as a result.

DIV returns the whole integer result of a division calculation if the remainder is discarded. 13 divided by 2 using the MOD operation would return 6.

```
INPUT HeightOfRectangle
INPUT WidthOfRectangle
AREA= HeightOfRectangle * WidthOfRectangle
DISPLAY AREA
END
```

Recognise this from the pseudocode section? The * shows that the two variables must be multiplied together.

```
INPUT Total Score
INPUT NumberOfStudents
AVERAGE= Total Score / NumberOfStudents
DISPLAY AVERAGE
END
```

This is an example of 'real' division: the result of the calculation could include decimal places. The **/** shows that the two variables must be divided.

```
INPUT Total Score
INPUT NumberOfStudents
AVERAGE= int(Total Score / NumberOfStudents)
DISPLAY AVERAGE
END
```

This is an example of 'integer': the result of the calculation will not include decimal places. The **int** shows that the remainder must be 'thrown away'.

Relational

The most common **relational** operators are ones you will remember from maths.
The symbols we use vary from language to language, but in pseudocode they are:

Action	Symbol
equal to	= or ==
not equal to	≠ or != or <>
less than	<
greater than	>
less than or equal to	<=
greater than or equal to	>=

```
INPUT TotalScore
INPUT NumberOfStudents
AVERAGE= int(TotalScore/NumberOfStudents)
IF AVERAGE > = 50
      OUTPUT "We did it!"
ELSE
      OUTPUT "We need to try again."
ENDIF
END
```

Look at this. What would the program output be if the average was 51?

KEYWORDS

Arithmetic ➤ The calculation using formulae and/or functions within a program

Relational ➤ Comparing two variables to come to a conclusion and act upon this

Boolean operators ➤ Used to narrow or expand a search by combining or excluding keywords

Boolean

You only need the most basic **Boolean operators**: **NOT**, **AND**, and **OR**. What might be new for computer science is that you need to be able to combine these terms.

Term	Result
AND	Both things must apply
OR	One or the other must apply
NOT	Neither one can apply

```
INPUT StudentScores
INPUT NumberOfStudents
HIGHSCORE = MAXIMUM (StudentScores)
LOWSCORE = MINIMUM (StudentScores)
AVERAGE= int(StudentScores/NumberOfScores)
IF HIGHSCORE > 85 OR AVERAGE > = 50
        OUTPUT "We did it!"
ELSE
        OUTPUT "Not so good."
ENDIF
END
```

See how the inclusion of OR changes the output of this code.

```
INPUT StudentScores
INPUT NumberOfStudents
HIGHSCORE = MAXIMUM (StudentScores)
LOWSCORE = MINIMUM (StudentScores)
AVERAGE= int(StudentScores/NumberOfScores)
IF HIGHSCORE > 85 AND AVERAGE > = 50
        OUTPUT "We did it!"
ELSE
        OUTPUT "Not so good."
ENDIF
END
```

See how the inclusion of AND makes this code more specific.

```
INPUT StudentScores
INPUT NumberOfStudents
HIGHSCORE = MAXIMUM (StudentScores)
LOWSCORE = MINIMUM (StudentScores)
AVERAGE= int(StudentScores / NumberOfScores)
IF HIGHSCORE > 85 NOT AVERAGE > = 50
        OUTPUT "That's quite a range of scores!"
ELSE
        OUTPUT "Not so big a range."
ENDIF
END
```

See how the inclusion of NOT changes the output of this code because the average must NOT be greater than or equal to 50.

Combinations

Natural English	Pseudocode	Result

If it's raining AND a school day OR I have to go to work I'll take the bus, otherwise I'll walk.	IF Raining AND SchoolDay OR WorkDay
	    TakeTheBus
	ELSE
	    Walk
	ENDIF
		Raining is the main component, then the decision is whether you are going to work *or* school.

If it's NOT raining AND a school day OR I have to go to work I'll walk, otherwise I'll take the bus.	IF NOT Raining AND SchoolDay OR WorkDay
	    Walk
	ELSE
	    TakeTheBus
	ENDIF
		This time, if it is not raining or you have to go to work or school, you'll take the bus, else you'll walk.

1. How would the results differ when using the MOD and DIV operators to calculate 11/2?
2. What is the computer output from the calculation (5+2) * (12/3)?
3. Write the pseudocode structure for a decision to have a cold drink if the temperature outside is hot, and a hot drink if not.

Flowcharts

Flowcharts are used to show the stages in a process or algorithm. A flowchart is used in other areas than computing because it clearly communicates a process without needing specialised jargon.

The code development process usually includes creation of a flowchart since it enables the coder to 'see' how the code should operate, which bits should go first, which bits can be looped and so on.

The main components

Shape	Purpose/Meaning
START/STOP	This is a **terminator** and you use it literally at the start and end of the flowchart to indicate where the whole code starts and finishes.
(process box)	This is a **process box**, one of the most frequently used shapes to indicate what the computer is doing.
(decision box)	This is the **decision box**, asking a question with multiple outcomes. They are most commonly used with a 'yes/no' or 'true/false' test but more than two choices can be offered in a more complex flowchart.
(parallelogram)	A parallelogram is used to represent the **input** or **output** of data in a process.
A A	Sometimes your flowchart is simply too big to fit on one page – these connectors are used to transfer the reader and flowchart from one page to the next, linking the letters so that the A of one page overlaps the A of the next to extend the flowchart.
→	An arrow shows the direction of travel of the data and the program.

Examples of simple flowcharts

Often the easiest way to understand something is to see it in action. Deciding whether to wear sunglasses to school can be shown as a simple flowchart:

KEYWORDS

Flowchart ➤ A visual way to map step-by-step decisions. The flow of logic and potential results in a system

Make a set of flowchart symbols using coloured paper and test each other on what each one means. Use sticky notes or sticky tape to create flowcharts on walls or doors.

1. Design a simple flowchart showing how to make tea and coffee.
2. Design a simple flowchart that shows the decision to take an umbrella if it is raining, but to leave it behind if it is not.
3. Design a simple flowchart to work out whether you can stay in bed for an extra hour, or have to go to school/college/work.

Programming 1

Fundamentals of programming

- **Concepts**
  - Iteration – e.g. rinse and repeat
    - Definite – set and never changes
    - Indefinite – changes depending on other conditions
  - Selection
    - e.g. IF kettle boiling THEN turn off kettle ELSE leave heat on
  - Nesting
    - Putting one element inside another
- **Statement types**
  - Variable declaration
    - Defines the variable
    - Variables can change value
  - Constant declaration
    - Defines the constant variable or name
    - Constants never change
  - Assignment
    - The method of naming a constant or variable
    - Often use = sign
  - Milestone 2
    - Many languages require this at the start of code
- **Data types**
  - Integer – e.g. 452
  - Boolean – e.g. on/off
  - Real – e.g. 17.5
  - Character – e.g. Y
  - String – e.g. Alex
  - Sequence – e.g. 1,2,3,4,5

- **Phase 3**
  - Top priorities
  - Mid priorities
  - Low priorities
- **Milestone 3**
  - Real
  - Modular or integer (with remainders)
- **Arithmetic**
  - Addition
  - Subtraction
  - Multiplication
  - Division

Arithmetic/ Relations/ Boolean

- **Relational**
  - Equal to
  - Not equal to
  - Less than
  - Greater than
  - Less than or equal to
  - Greater than or equal to
- **Boolean**
  - Not
  - And
  - Or
  - A combination of the three

Pseudocode

- **What?**
  - Shared language
  - Based on English
  - Easy to understand
  - Allows easy reading by others
- **Why?**
  - Useful as part of planning process
  - Shows structure of code before write-up
- **Characteristics**
  - Always starts with the name of the program
  - Always ends with END
  - Each statement on a separate line
  - Indent loops and IF or WHILE sections
  - No fixed syntax
  - Arrows show data flow

If you need more space to answer the following questions, please use a separate piece of paper.

1. Look at the code below, and answer the questions that follow:

```
Counter = 0
WHILE counter < 11:
        Counter +=1
        PRINT counter
PRINT "All done".
```

   a) What data type is 'counter'? **(1 mark)**

   _____

   b) Define the terms below referring to the code:

      i) Variable **(1 mark)**

      _____

      _____

      ii) Iteration **(1 mark)**

      _____

      _____

      iii) Algorithm **(1 mark)**

      _____

      _____

2. Why is it good practice to use appropriately named subroutines, constants and variables? **(2 marks)**

_____

_____

3. What is meant by 'assignment of variables'? **(1 mark)**

_____

_____

4. Describe what the difference is between definite and indefinite iteration. **(2 marks)**

_____

_____

_____

5. Give a pseudocode example of nested selection. **(3 marks)**

_____

_____

_____

6. What is the difference between AND and NOT Boolean operators? **(1 mark)**

_____

Exam practice questions

Programming 1

Data structure types

Data structures in computer science allow us to store multiple pieces of data that are used in programs. In pseudocode, and in many programming languages, arrays are indicated by [], as in ClassGroup = [Alex, Bailey, Krishna, Jamie, Riley].

The main data types are:

Array – An array is a collection of something: for example, students in a class. Only one type of data can be stored in an array – if you want to mix, say, names and numbers you would have to use a list. You only need to worry about two different types of array: **one-dimensional** and **two-dimensional**.

Records – This is a term you will have met in your study of databases. A record is a single instance within an array (or database), so one student's information within a class database would be one record. A record is used to hold different pieces of data about one item.

Uses of arrays

A simple array could be the names of students in a group:
ClassGroup = [Alex, Bailey, Krishna, Jamie, Riley]
And now you could change things on this group as one group, rather than having to operate on each individual separately, such as moving them from Year 10 to Year 11, or from Ms Smith's class to Mr Hussain's class.

A two-dimensional array could be your class timetable or book reviews by different students, so that each row is a different book, and each column is the review by a different student. Now you can see how each book is reviewed by a lot of reviewers, or the type of book a particular reviewer liked.

	Alex	Bailey	Krishna	Jamie	Riley
Jane Eyre	5	6	2	1	2
Of Mice and Men	6	4	5	3	4
Flowers for Algernon	9	5	5	1	6

We could work out from this that Jamie maybe doesn't like reading at all and that the most popular book is *Flowers for Algernon*. You can also see the **record structure**, the template for data storage that will most effectively do whatever you need. In this case, entries cover what the readers have read and the names of the readers: the table structure above does that.

Often this form of structure will include **key fields** which are uniquely attached to each record, so that if there were two students named Alex who read *Of Mice and Men*, we would know that this Alex was the one we were looking for, because the key field is different.

In your school records, you will have a UPN, a Unique Pupil Number. This is your key field, or primary key. Even if someone was born on the same day as you, with the same name and address, they couldn't be mixed up with you.

Data structures

Module 8

Accessing items in an array

One-dimensional array

In a **one-dimensional** array you can access any one of the contents by identifying its position within the array – remembering that the numbers start at 0! So:

Score = [2,4,6,8,10]
Output score[2]

Will show 6, because 2 is at position 0, 4 is at position 1, and 6 is at position 2.

You can use a loop to update simple arrays, and cover each of item in turn:

```
HIGH = 0
FOR EACH SCORE
        IF SCORE > HIGH
        HIGH = SCORE
END
```

Or you can use a specific index point (*i* in this example) to access specific items within the array:

HIGH = 0 ← 0 is the first position, but you could start further into the array as I have here, by saying that you only want to work from position 5.

```
FOR I IN RANGE 5: (LENGTH OF SCORE) –
        IF HIGH < SCORE [I]:
        HIGH = SCORE [I]
END
```

Two-dimensional array

In a **two-dimensional** array you can also access items specifically, or traverse the entire array. On a chess board, the array would be defined as BOARD [8,8] because there are 8 spaces in each row, and 8 rows. Now you can identify where each piece would be by identifying its row and column. Computers use this form of reference to create the images you see on your computer, phone and television screen: each pixel is defined separately.

Now to update the data for the reading scores table at the start of this section (Krishna now rated *Jane Eyre* 5, as well as the other books) you would identify the row and column:

BookScore [0] [2] = 5

		0	1	2	3
		Alex	Bailey	Krishna	Jamie
0	*Jane Eyre*	5	6	5	1
1	*Of Mice and Men*	6	4	5	3
2	*Flowers for Algernon*	9	5	5	1

Make your fridge into a two-dimensional array. Sort your fridge shelves into 'dairy' on one shelf, 'fruit/vegetables' on another shelf, and so on.

1. What would be an example of a record in a doctors' surgery database?
2. What would be in an array of pet names?
3. How could you make a one-dimensional array of pet names into a two-dimensional array that would identify the pet type?

Input/output and file handling

Input/output and file handling is a technical way of describing what happens in most programs: some data is input, something happens to it, and the result is output.

Think about this example:

| Student name entered **(INPUT)** | ▶ | Saved onto a file called THISFORM **(FILE HANDLING)** | ▶ | Printed onto a register list for fire drill **(OUTPUT)** |

Your code needs to be able to handle this sort of task. You need to be able to gain input from the user when you need it – from a keyboard for example – process it, and output a result of the processing. Usually, as part of your coursework, you need to be able to handle a text file. Often these will be in **.csv** or **.txt** format.

One way of handling files is to create one from your first entries:

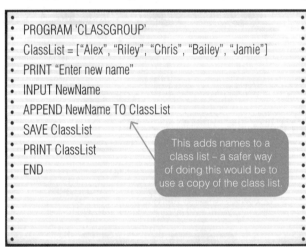

```
PROGRAM 'CLASSGROUP'
ClassList = ["Alex", "Riley", "Chris", "Bailey", "Jamie"]
PRINT "Enter new name"
INPUT NewName
APPEND NewName TO ClassList
SAVE ClassList
PRINT ClassList
END
```

This adds names to a class list – a safer way of doing this would be to use a copy of the class list.

Often files already exist, and need updating rather than creating. In this case, the code above wouldn't work because it could repeatedly overwrite existing names.

```
PROGRAM 'CLASSGROUP'
ClassList = ["Alex", "Riley", "Chris", "Bailey", "Jamie"]
PRINT "Enter new name or x to exit"
INPUT NewName
IF NewName = = ClassList
        PRINT "Name already exists"
ELSE
        IF NewName NOT x
        APPEND NewName TO ClassList
SAVEAS ClassList2
PRINT ClassList2
END
```

This would open an original file, and update the data with new names into a new file, with the user able to use x to exit the program.

Processes

Opening a file: If you are to access the contents, rather like using clothes in a suitcase, you need to open it. In most cases, you also need to identify how you plan to use it once it is open.

WORK = OPEN(CLASSLIST.csv, r) ←

> Opening the class list just to **read** it: maybe I am checking that the list is up to date.

WORK = OPEN(CLASSLIST.csv, w) ←

> Opening the class list to **write** to it: the old list will be replaced with this one.

WORK = OPEN(CLASSLIST.csv, a) ←

> Opening the class list just to **append** data to it: there is a new student who must be added.

WORK = OPEN(CLASSLIST.csv, r+) ←

> Opening the class list to **read AND write** to it. This is most convenient – but if you write to it you replace the old one!

Considering the example of a class list shown above, the reason for accessing the data will decide on whether to open the file in **read**, **write**, **append** or **read and write** mode.

Simply reading from a file can be done by displaying each line number from the first to the last in a FOR loop.

```
OPEN (ClassList.csv,r)
FOR Eachline IN ClassList.csv
    OUTPUT Eachline
END
```

Use shoeboxes and toilet rolls to create an INPUT – PROCESS (and storage) – OUTPUT model. You can roll marbles from one shoebox through to the other to demonstrate the process.

1. What is the difference between opening a file with write access and opening a file with read access?
2. Why wouldn't you just open all files read and write access?

String handling

Handling **strings** refers to 'groups' of characters. There are a range of operations that you might need to perform on strings:

- length ➤ the number of characters.
- position ➤ the location of a specified substring.
- **substring** ➤ any contiguous sequence of characters within a string.
- **concatenation** ➤ the joining of strings end-to-end.
- convert character to character code ➤ conversion to ASCII code and back again for example.
- string conversion operations ➤ changing letters from uppercase to lowercase for example.

A string is a sequence of characters in memory, just like a piece of string.

What are strings used for?

Strings are any sequence of characters, anything from phone numbers to essays, class lists to email addresses. Manipulating them is a central task for most computer languages.

An important characteristic of each string is its length, which is the number of characters in it. The length can be any whole number or integer.

A particularly useful string for some programming applications is the empty string, which is a string containing no characters and thus having a length of 0. Programmers can set up this string for error conditions, for example, and set a test of looking for whenever that string is greater in length than 0.

In Python version 3 and above, you can see we have two strings below, and I am asking it to identify a specific location in each one – position [0] in string 1 (i.e. the first character) and positions [1:5] in the second (characters 2 through 6).

```
var1 = "Hello World!"
var2 = "Python Language Study"
print("var1[0]: ", var1[0])
print("var2[1:5], ", var2[1:5])
```

When the above code is run,
it produces the following result:

```
var1[0]: H
var2[1:5]: ytho
```

KEYWORDS

String ➤ A sequence of characters, such as a name or telephone number

Substring ➤ Any identified single sequence of characters in a string

Concatenation ➤ Joining two strings together end-to-end to create one longer string; 'Sun' and 'shine', for example, would become 'sunshine'

10

Task	Pseudocode examples	Action
Return the length of a string	Stringname.length OR LEN(stringname)	How long is the string? For example, how many students in a class? (Remember strings start at position 0.) someText="Computer Science" print(someText.length) (*OCR*)
Return the position in a string	String.indexOf(n)	Looks at the *n*th entry in a file (indexing starts at position 1) if contents of file fruit.txt is: L1 orange L2 banana L3 grape line2 ← READLINE(fruit.txt, 2) # line2 is "L2 banana"
Return the substring data within the string	Stringname. SubString(startingPosition, numberOfCharacters)	Substrings start with the 0th character, and will 'chop' strings into smaller groups: CutText="Computer Science" print(CutText.substring(3,3) will display 'put'
Concatenation of two strings	String.Join OR NewString = String1 + String2 Can also sometimes include: , and &	Appends one string to another to make a longer string. if contents of file fruit.txt is: L1 apple L2 banana L3 clementine and contents of file veg.txt is: S1 potatoes S2 celery S3 pepper Then shopping.txt = fruit.txt + veg.txt to create a shopping list that includes both entries. **note + does not work as a mathematical function**
Convert string to integer	Int(string)	Changes the string into an integer. You might need this if you are working out ages or scores.
Convert integer to string	Str(integer)	Turns the integer into a string – such as a telephone number.
Convert string to real	Float(string)	You may remember about 'floating' decimal places – 'float' is also a Python command you might recognise.
Convert real to string	Str(variable)	You can also change the decimal number into a string, such as an IP address.
Convert content of string to upper case	String.toUpper(inString)	Changes to content of the string to all upper case letters.
Convert content of string to lower case	String.toLower(inString)	Changes the content of the string to all lower case letters.
Comparison of content of two strings	Strcmp(string1,string2)	This is a Boolean comparison, returning 1 if identical and 0 if not.

Use different colour threads to create a literal string and show how APPEND or + can extend the string.

1. Create a table that shows the commands to change one piece of data (such as a weight or date of birth) into different data types.
2. Think of two different reasons why knowing the ASCII code of a character would be useful.
3. If a textfile contains 'GCSE Computer Science' what would be output by print(textfile.substring(13,3)?

Random number generation

Truly random numbers are hard to come by for humans: we tend to stick to patterns. When we talk about random numbers we are often really referring to chance – that there is a uniform distribution of, say, flowers in a meadow. Of course, this isn't really the case, because the flowers will go where the conditions are best, rather than spacing themselves out evenly.

Computers use random numbers in commercial, educational and scientific systems across the world; from gaming, cryptography, gambling and medical simulations. A series of truly random numbers could be of any size and extremely difficult for a computer to reproduce. **Pseudorandom** numbers are computer generated and calculated to appear to be random but are repeatable.

Selecting random numbers

In pseudocode, random numbers are selected using the term RANDOM

Var <– Random(1–100) would produce a random number within the range 1–100

In Python version 3, the code looks like:

```
#Random Number between 1 and 100
import random
print (random.randrange(1,100))
```

Secure encryption and random numbers

Encryption services, used in everything from banking to private messaging systems, scramble data so that it can only be read with an associated encryption key. The algorithms that generate these keys use random numbers or, more specifically, pseudorandom numbers to prevent them from being calculated by those wanting to crack the encryption.

KEYWORDS

Pseudorandom ➤ Number selection that follows a rule rather than offering numbers on a truly random basis

1. Identify industries where pseudorandom numbers are used.
2. Why could a truly random number generator cause problems for a programmer?

Use numbered ping pong balls to create your own random and pseudorandom number generator. (Remember to put the selected ping pong ball back for random numbers.)

Introduction to databases

Relational databases hold data in a **structured** format that allows it to be readily searched and processed by the computer using algorithms. A good example of structured data is data held on a spreadsheet where every cell is addressable and identifiable and data can be sorted by multiple criteria. In databases, however, the structures are clear: called records and **fields**, they manage the data in a fashion that allows the program to search, update and edit, delete and report back on the contents in a speedy and effective way.

SQL (Structured Query Language) is a language designed to work with relational databases.

In simple terms, **unstructured** data is the opposite. Computers are not as effective at dealing with unstructured data: this is something humans do better. An example of unstructured data is the content of an email message, which is difficult to categorise into a table.

Components of databases

Databases have two main elements: the part that actually holds the data and the **DBMS** (database management system) that is used by applications to access that data. It is the DBMS that enforces the structure, ensuring that:

➤ all relationships between data are maintained (so everyone who started the day in class 7W ends the day in class 7W unless there's a deliberate action to move them)

➤ all data is stored correctly and rules are not violated (so no one in class 7W is 64-years-old)

➤ all data is recoverable to a safe point in the case of a disaster (keeping backups).

Although there are a number of different ways to organise data, over time **relational databases** have proved to be one of the most powerful. In relational databases, data is held in tables which represent a set of items such as employees. Each table is constructed in columns and rows:

> Each of the titles here refers to a field within the table.

> This is a single table from inside the students' database.

> This is a unique number allocated to this student record only.

> This is a field from inside the students' database.

Students' database – record for Alex Hussain

Field name	Example content
UniquePupilNumber (UPN)	AS3Q87FH912WW
FirstName	Alex
LastName	Hussain
Sex	F
DateOfBirth (dd/mm/yyyy)	01/01/2005
FirstLineOfAddress	1, CherryTree Lane
LastLineOfAddress	Bramley
PostCode	ZZ12 2ZZ
FormGroup	EH

You can see a UniquePupilNumber is allocated to every student. This means that no matter how many Alex Hussains there are in the school, or in the country, this one is the only one with that number, so we can use that number to check we are using the correct data.

1. What is the relationship between Alex's FormGroup entry and the FormGroup table?
2. What is the difference between a record and a field?

Module 12 Databases

The technical name for the field that we guarantee is unique to each record is **primary key**. Often when designing database tables, we will include an ID field automatically, and relational database programs such as Microsoft Access© automatically include this field whenever you create a table.

So far this table has very little detail. The rest of Alex's class could be added without a common link but these would be contained in unrelated tables. A new table called FormGroups could be set up with the FormGroup (EH) field used as a link between them. Links between tables using common fields are the power of relational databases.

When more than one table is used then **foreign keys** can appear; this is a field in one table but also a primary key in another. In the case of Alex, her UPN is a primary key in this table, but might be also included in a class table for each of her subject classes, so would be a foreign key in those tables.

ENGLISH CLASS STUDENTNUMBER (fkey)	←	ALEX HUSSAIN UPN AS3Q87FH912WW (pkey)	→	SCIENCE CLASS STUDENTNUMBER (fkey)

Relationships in a relational database

There are three relationships within a relational database:

One-to-one – This is when each entry in our student table has only one relationship in another table. Generally, we don't use one-to-one relationships much because if there is only one link, that data could often be held on the single table.

One-to-many – This is the most common type of relationship: each record in one table links to one or more records in another table, but each record in the second table links to only one record in the first table. Looking at Alex's table, while she has only one form group, that form group will have more than one student.

Many-to-many – This is when each record in one table links to one or more in the second, and vice versa. An example here would be Alex's teachers: each teacher may teach more than one subject and each subject may be taught by more than one teacher.

Setting up these tables is an art in itself of **decomposition**: breaking down a task into smaller tasks so that a computer can process more effectively. This also applies to databases – in this context you decompose your data into multiple tables, to limit duplication of data entry and storage as far as possible.

KEYWORDS

Structured ➤ Some sort of organisation

Field ➤ A single unit of data stored about an entity, stored with other fields to create a record. An example would be 'name'

SQL ➤ Structured Query Language, used to process the data held in relational databases

Unstructured ➤ No clear method of organising to the level of structured data

DBMS ➤ Database Management System

Relational database ➤ A database that holds data in a structured format identifying links between fields

Primary key ➤ A field with contents unique to each record, enabling otherwise identical data records to still be separated and processed accurately, such as an account number

Foreign key ➤ A foreign key is a primary key in one table, and included in another linked table

Decomposition ➤ You decompose your data into multiple tables, to limit duplication of data entry and storage as far as possible

Programming 2

Random number generator
- Description
- Key stakeholders
- Background
- Input/output
  - Input usually from a keyboard only
  - Output to screen or printer
  - Read from and write to a text file
  - .csv files – comma separated values
- File handling
- File types
  - .txt files – text files
- Team manager
- Project manager

String handling
- Length
- Substrings
- Position
- Concatenation
- Conversion
  - String/Integer
  - Real/String
- Input usually from a keyboard only

String handling
- Length
- Substrings
- Position
- Concatenation
- Conversion
  - String/Integer
  - Real/String

Data structures
- Records
  - Single instance in an array
- Arrays
  - One-dimensional – list
  - Two-dimensinal – table

Input/output, file handling
- Input/output
- File handling
- File types
- Output to screen or printer
- Read from and write to a text file
- .csv files – comma separated values

If you need more space to answer the following questions, please use a separate piece of paper.

1. Describe the difference between a one-dimensional array and a two-dimensional array, with an example. **(4 marks)**

_____

_____

_____

_____

_____

_____

2. Read and answer the questions about the following table in a relational database.

Employee number	LastName	Rank	Room	Shift
2570	Smith	Manager	A1	Day
1010	Jones	Site staff	W4	Afternoon
984	Hassan	Team leader	Q1	Day
299	Cengiz	Site staff	W4	Morning

a) Identify a record in this table. **(1 mark)**

_____

b) Which of the data would be best suited to being a primary key? Give a reason for your answer. **(2 marks)**

_____

_____

c) What would be a reasonable field size for LastName? Give a reason for your answer. **(2 marks)**

_____

_____

3. A programmer is developing a web-based lending library. She has to decide between using a text file and a relational database to store the data that is needed for the library stock.

Which would be the most appropriate and why? **(4 marks)**

_____

_____

_____

_____

4. In 7-bit ASCII, what is this message?

01000001 01010011 01000011 01001001 01001001 00001010 01000011

01001111 01000100 01000101 **(3 marks)**

_____

5. What limitation of ASCII is overcome by Unicode? **(2 marks)**

_____

_____

Subroutines and structured programming

13

Subroutines are blocks of code that can be put anywhere in a program and are 'called' in the body of the code just by naming them. Functions and procedures are both examples of subroutines; a function returns a value, a procedure does not – it performs a task, but doesn't send any result back to the user.

They are both part of a whole approach to coding called **structured programming**.

> Code written without subroutines is often called 'spaghetti code' because it is so much longer!

> Breaking any big task into little ones (decomposition) makes it more achievable.

> Updating the code is made easier as subroutines can be edited individually.

> Why is structured programming so helpful?

> Using code modules or subroutines (one for each part of the task) makes it easy to see which part of the code does a specific task.

Advantages of subroutines
Iteration: the code can be written once, then used again. An example of this is the drain or spin cycle on a washing machine: only written once, but used a number of times. In the controller code, there will be one set of instructions to control the action, often either at the start or end of the main code, and within the main code there will be the instruction 'spin' or 'drain' and this will call that subroutine into play.
Keeps code shorter because you are only writing the code once for the subroutine. No matter how many times you need it, your code can be considerably shorter.
Easier to test large tasks, if decomposed into smaller subtasks. Can be easy to test one module – or subroutine – at a time.
You can access and use any variable from your main code without having to redefine it, so if we use the spin cycle example again, the SpinSpeed variable might be 800 rpm at one point in the program, and the subroutine will use that. Then, when the controller returns to the main code after running that subroutine, SpinSpeed might be increased to 1200 – and the subroutine will use that.

Programmers take note:	
When using structured programming and subroutines it's important to remember the following:	• Code using subroutines isn't linear so they can be placed at any point within a program.
	• Subroutines need to be clearly identifiable.
	• Planning ahead is really important.

Translators – usually included within programming software – convert **high-level language** into **low-level language** (machine code). There are three types of translator: assemblers, interpreters or compilers.

	Purpose	Advantages	Disadvantages
Assembler	An assembler translates assembly language into machine code (also known as source code).	This is far closer to the machine code, so there are fewer errors in translation.	Very device specific with limited instructions available. More difficult to code and complex tasks require long programs.
Compiler	A compiler translates the whole program that the programmer has written into machine code in one sweep before the program is run.	This is much faster than running interpreted code, since once it has been compiled it is done.	It can be difficult to test individual lines of compiled code compared to interpreted languages because you only get to know the errors after the whole program has been compiled.
Interpreter	An interpreter **translates code written by programmers into machine code, instruction by instruction as the computer operates it,** not all at once.	Interpreted code will show an error as soon as it hits a problem, so it is easier to **debug** than **compiled** code.	Running this can take a lot longer than compiled code, and since the code is interpreted one line at a time, each time you run it you have to interpret it again.

Modern washing machines are controlled by a computer, using subroutines to automate the elements of each wash cycle.

KEYWORDS

High-level language ➤ Programming languages that resemble natural language in their structure and syntax. Examples include Java and Python. For a computer to understand and run it the program must be compiled into machine language

Low-level language ➤ Written to provide instructions directly to a processor. Examples include assembly and machine code and although fast and efficient they are difficult to learn

Watch or record yourself or a friend walking and running to see how these activities are also made up of subroutines.

1. A games console, for example, will use subroutines to open the disc tray, turn on LED lights or play a jingle when turned on. Can you identify other household appliances or devices that also use subroutines?
2. For each of the devices or appliances you have listed, what operations might the subroutines do? Use the games console example to guide you.

Parameters

In strictly formal terms a **parameter** is a variable. They are sometimes called **arguments**.

In pseudocode, the general practice is that subroutines are kept at the end of the code. The syntax for subroutines is straightforward: programs always begin with 'program name' and subroutines start with either <sub> or <proc> (or <procedure>) followed by its name and **parameters**.

```
SUB NAME (parameters)
     do something
ENDSUB
```

The parameter defines how the rest of the subroutine operates.

Example:

If a tree grows 20 cm per year, then the subroutine for calculating the height of the tree would be Height(AgeOfTree) = 20 * (AgeOfTree). The '20' is the parameter: it controls the rest of the process.

A more mathematical example could be to draw a graph showing the grades achieved by a class of students:
SUB Graph(x,y)
Where the x and y values are set or calculated elsewhere in the program.

When a subroutine has input parameters like the examples above, the output of the subroutine is often affected by the values that are passed into the function. So a single subroutine can be called many times within a program and produce a different result each time. A more complicated example can be seen if we go back to the washing machine code:

```
PROGRAM "WashingMachine";
Check WaterLevel
IF WaterLevel = Top
      WashCycle
ELSE
      Fill
ENDIF

WashCycle
SpinSpeed = 800
SpinCycle
RinseCycle
SpinSpeed = 1200
SpinCycle
END
```

Filling the washing machine with water – without overfilling!

Calling the WashCycle at this point in the code – but it is written separately at the end.

```
SUB WashCycle
      WHILE Timer <10
      Turn drum right 30 secs
      Turn drum left 30 secs
      ENDWHILE
ENDSUB

SUB SpinCycle (SpinSpeed)
      Turn pump ON
      Int (SpinSpeed)
      Spin (SpinSpeed)
      IF pump dry
            Stop spin
      ELSE
            SpinCycle
      ENDIF
ENDSUB
```

Once the WashCycle is done, the controller returns to the main code for its next instruction – which sets the spin speed and sends it off to find the SpinCycle subroutine. When it returns it is sent off again to the RinseCycle, then back, resets to a higher spin speed to do the SpinCycle yet again, and back again to finish.

SpinCycle is its own subroutine – and you can see how the parameter SpinSpeed is used differently before and after rinsing. SpinSpeed has been set to INT just in case anything went adrift earlier on and I'm asking the motor to spin at a speed that includes a decimal place.

```
SUB RinseCycle
      Check WaterLevel
      IF WaterLevel = Top
              WHILE Timer <10
              Turn drum right 30 secs
              Turn drum left 30 secs
              ENDWHILE
      ELSE
      Fill
      ENDIF
ENDSUB
END
```

Rinse Cycle, in this case, is just ONE rinse, but modern machines have a different final rinse that often includes fabric softener.

It can sometimes be problematic to use a variable from outside the subroutine (or **global** variable) so sometimes a subroutine will use its own variables, such as the timer in the washing machine example. This is called a **local** variable and is sometimes more reliable since it is only used and defined inside that subroutine and not affected by anything from the rest of the code.

Local variables are just used in the function where they have been declared, and once the program comes to an end, the local variable is erased from computer memory.

Global variables are usually defined at the start of a program, outside of any function. They can be called or accessed from any function or subroutine at any point of the program.

Use parameters to define how a friend moves or performs a task – tidying their room angrily or brushing their hair twenty times, for example.

1. In the washing machine code, is the WaterLevel variable global or local?
2. Why are global variables sometimes problematic?

Validation and authentication

To make your code robust and secure, you need to be able to include **validation** and **authentication** routines as part of your process.

Validation

Validation checks what you need to know, include:

➤ Checking that a user has entered any data
➤ Checking that data entered is within a set range

> It doesn't check that you are telling the truth – just that you know the answer it is looking for! Checking for the truth is **verification**

15

Verification checks what you need to know, including:

➤ Double entry – entering the data twice – often by two different people to ensure no crossover – and comparing the two copies. This effectively doubles the workload, and costs more too.
➤ Proofreading data – this method involves someone checking the data entered against the original document. This is also time consuming and costly.

Suppose I am creating a social media site and I want to make sure that no one aged under 13 takes part. The simplest way of setting this up looks something like:

```
PROGRAM 'AGECHECK'
OUTPUT "ENTER YOUR AGE"
IF AGE => 13
    OUTPUT "WELCOME!"
ELSE
    OUTPUT "TOO YOUNG!"
END
```

Authentication

The only authentication checks that you need to know focus on are **username** and **password**.

Simple WHILE routines would ensure that your code fulfils this requirement.

```
USERNAME = "FRED"
OUTPUT "ENTER YOUR USERNAME"
WHILE USERNAME ≠ "FRED"
    OUTPUT "INCORRECT USERNAME"
ENDWHILE
OUTPUT "WELCOME, FRED!"
END
```

Testing

Testing takes place after creating any program to see if it meets its original specification and is fully functional. This is done through using test data from across the expected range as well as invalid data.

You **must** use a clear range of test data, and **be able to justify your choices**.

Type of test data	Example (checking age between 13 and 19)	Reasoning
Normal or typical	15, 18	Part of the 'normal' range and should be accepted. Tests that the original check was set up accurately.
Extreme or boundary	14, 19	Right at the edge of the range, so checks that you've used => rather than just >.
Erroneous (or invalid)	FRED	Checks that the code is strong enough to withstand input that results if the user is malicious or is not paying attention.

There are three types of error you may encounter:

SYNTAX errors	These occur when the programmer fails to obey one of the grammar rules of the programming language they are using. This could be putting capital letters where they don't belong.
RUNTIME errors	A program running that comes across a problem it cannot resolve will throw, or stop with, a runtime error. Programming errors, hardware malfunctions or errors when accessing computer memory can cause this.
LOGIC errors	These can be the most difficult kind of errors to detect and fix, because often there is no obvious error within the code. The program will run successfully, but will produce incorrect results.

Language classification

There are a range of programming languages, all of which fit into two categories:

High-level languages are closest to human language, and are the most recently developed. They need a compiler because the computer doesn't understand them.

Low-level languages are closest to the way the computer operates, with direct commands the computer understands.

High-level languages	Low-level languages
Easier to read because they are close to human language.	Hard to read because they are closer to computer code than human language.
Most code is written in these because they can be designed for a specific purpose and are easier to use.	Only specific tasks are written in these because they are complex to operate.
Easier to learn because they are closer to the way we speak.	Harder to learn because they are not in a familiar structure.
Used to control software more than hardware: you can control many computers using the same language.	Used to control hardware rather than software: you need to know the computer for which you are coding.
Examples: Java, Visual Basic, BASIC, the C family, Pascal, Python.	Examples: machine code is the lowest level language, and the only one that the computer can handle without any intervention. The next is assembly language, which is a little closer to human language. True machine code is binary!

Each processor (or chip) has its own machine code instruction set, which is why if you want to use machine code you have to know the machine! The few people who still use assembly language are those who work in designing software for **embedded systems** (such as a sat nav in a car) or for controlling specific hardware, such as writing device drivers.

KEYWORDS

Validation ➤ Checks that data is reasonable, within any set limits. It does not check that something is 'true'

Authentication ➤ The process of identifying a user accessing a system or program, normally through a username and password

Verification ➤ Checks that something is true. This is hard for a computer to do, since as yet we do not have reliable ways to tell if someone is being honest

Embedded systems ➤ A computer system with a dedicated function within a larger system, typically an electrical or mechanical system

1. The code below checks for an age entry of greater than 13.

```
PROGRAM 'AGECHECK'
OUTPUT "ENTER YOUR AGE"
IF AGE>13
    OUTPUT "WELCOME!"
ELSE
    OUTPUT "TOO YOUNG!"
END
```

a) Change this to look for a date of birth instead of a set age.
b) What difference would be made if you changed the IF statement to 'IF AGE =>13'?
c) Note how this automatically checks for no entry at all. How does this show the weakness of this sort of validation?

Programming 3

Subroutines

Advantages
- Iteration
- Enscapulation
- Easier to test individual sections
- Use variables set elsewhere in the code

Disadvantages
- Much more self-discipline needed
- Sometimes harder to read
- Sometimes takes more coding than simple code
- Demands more computer power
- Control how a subroutine operates

Use parameters

Robust and secure programming
- Validation – checks data is within range
- Verification – checks data is true
- Authentication – checks a user enters the right data to confirm their identity/access rights

Structures programming

Means decomposing large tasks into smaller ones and coding each small task separately

Advantages
- Easier to complete the big task through smaller, interim ones
- Modules or subroutines signpost what part of the code meets each function
- Updates can be local – just the subroutine that needs to be replaced

Disadvantages
- Code jumps about so need to be exact about references
- Parameters can be unreliable if variables/parameters are changed by the main code
- Takes a lot of testing

Language classification

High-level
- Close to human language
- Easier to read
- Slower in operation because computer has to translate it
- Most common languages used
- Examples: Pascal, Python, Basic

Low-level
- Lowest machine code – binary
- 2nd lowest is assembly language – device drivers
- Not commonly used: dependent on knowing the device in use

Testing
- Normal data – within range
- Extreme or boundary data – at the edges but should still be accepted
- Erroneous data – rubbish!

If you need more space to answer the following questions, please use a separate piece of paper.

1. Explain the advantages of using subroutines in programs. **(4 marks)**

_____

_____

_____

_____

2. Explain the advantages of the structured approach to programming. **(3 marks)**

_____

_____

_____

3. Why is it good practice to use local variables? **(3 marks)**

_____

_____

_____

4. Describe the use of parameters to pass data within programs. **(3 marks)**

_____

_____

_____

5. What is the difference between data validation and data verification? **(4 marks)**

_____

_____

_____

_____

6. What rules should test data follow? Give reasons for your answer. **(6 marks)**

_____

_____

_____

_____

_____

7. Explain the main differences between low-level and high-level languages. **(6 marks)**

_____

_____

_____

_____

_____

Programming 3

Number bases

You need to be comfortable with three number bases:

1. **Decimal** (base 10)
2. **Binary** (base 2)
3. **Hexadecimal** (base 16)

Decimal is the base you will probably recognise most easily.

All computers use **binary** to function – computers are basically a set of switches which can be either 'on' or 'off', represented by 0 for 'off' and 1 for 'on'. Counting in binary is easy once you see the pattern. Most exam boards focus on **8-bit** structures, so we'll use that here. This means the highest numbers you will have to face are 255 in decimal, 1111 1111 in binary, or FF in hexadecimal – and you don't need to worry about decimal places.

Each **hexadecimal** digit represents 4 bits (or a **nibble**), so this is more human-friendly than binary.

Counting in the different bases

Whatever the base, when you are counting up you move one space to the left when you reach the number of that base. So we move to tens when we reach 10 in decimal, we move to 2 when we reach 2 in binary, we move to 16 when we reach 16 in hexadecimal. You need to be able to convert each of these bases into one of the others.

Predicting the sequence is easier if you look at each one in detail. Base 10 would look like:

10000000	1000000	100000	10000	1000	100	10	1

Each time the numbers move to the left, the value increases by a power of 10, so 10 is ten times 1, 100 is ten times 10, 1000 is ten times 100.

Base 2 looks like:

128	64	32	16	8	4	2	1

Each time the numbers move to the left, the value increases by a power of 2, so 2 is two times 1, 4 is two times 2, 8 is two times 4.

Base 16 looks like:

4096	256	16	1

Each time the numbers move to the left, the value increases by a power of 16, so 16 is sixteen times 1, 256 is sixteen times 16, 4096 is sixteen times 256.

Simple conversions in each base: side by side

Decimal	Binary	Hexadecimal
Whole decimal number **74**	Using base 10: {table} 64+8+2=74 **74 converted to binary: 01001010**	Using the first 3 base 16 blocks: {table} and the hexadecimal number system: 0,1,2,3,4,5,6,7,8,9,A,B,C,D,E,F. 256 is too high to use but 16 will go into 74. 74/16 = 4 with a remainder of 10. The number 10 is represented by A. 74 converted to hexadecimal is 4A

Binary table:

128	64	32	16	8	4	2	1
0	1	0	0	1	0	1	0

Hexadecimal table:

256	16	1

Binary arithmetic

Using the following rules, it is also possible to add 8-bit binary numbers together without converting to another format.

Consider the following addition: 0001 0101 + 0010 1001

Work from the right and follow these basic rules:

(0+0=0), (1+0=1), (0+1=1), (1+1=0 and carry 1) and (1+1+1=1 and carry 1)

```
            0 0 0 1 1 1 0 1
            0 0 0 1 1 0 0 1
            0 0 1 1 0 1 1 0
carry line:     1 1     1
```

We use **leading zeros** to show where the other digits are, to indicate that this is 8-bit binary.

Binary shift (arithmetic shift and logical shift)

A 'shift' moves the bits held in the **register** either to the left or right.

Arithmetic shift

Arithmetic shifts effectively divide the number by two for each step they shift right, or multiply the number by 2 for each step they shift left.

Shift left (multiply by 2):

256 (carry over)	128	64	32	16	8	4	2	1	Decimal
		1	1	0	1	1	1	1	0	222
1	1	0	1	1	1	1	0	0 *(new 0 to show shift left)*	188 (shift left) + 256 = 444

Shift right (divide by 2):

128	64	32	16	8	4	2	1	Decimal
1	1	0	1	1	1	1	0	222
	1	1	0	1	1	1	1 *(the old 0 shifted off the register)*	111

Logical shift

Logical shifts are more suited to logical functions and are more straightforward – bits which are shifted are lost (not carried over as in the example above) and the spaces created are filled with zeros.

Logical shift LEFT:

128	64	32	16	8	4	2	1
1	1	0	1	1	1	1	0
1	0	1	1	1	1	0	0 *(new 0 to show shift left)*

Logical shift RIGHT:

128	64	32	16	8	4	2	1
1	1	0	1	1	1	1	0
0 *(new 0 to show shift right)*	1	1	0	1	1	1	1

Examples here have been controlled to ensure that they don't fall victim to overflow: this is when the leftmost digit in binary arithmetic 'falls off' the end – in a 4-bit calculation, for example, when you would need a fifth bit (e.g. 8 + 8 = 16). When this occurs it sets a flag in the computer and the software has to deal with it because the result would simply be wrong otherwise. For us, doing binary arithmetic on paper, we identify that this would be an overflow result, and put the correct answer.

KEYWORDS

8-bit ➤ A 'bit' is a **b**inary dig**it** that holds either a '1' or a '0'. So 8-bit is 8 of these in a set together, also known as a byte

Nibble ➤ Another word for 4-bit

Leading zeros ➤ Zeros put in positions left blank to the left of the first digit (to indicate binary representation in this case), such as telephone numbers

Register ➤ A location in memory where data is stored

1. Identify one reason why programmers often use hexadecimal, instead of binary, to represent numbers.
2. Put these in the correct ascending sequence by size: byte, bit, nibble.
3. Add 00011010 + 0001001 in binary, and show the decimal answer.

Units of information

You need to remember the basics:

A **bit** is the fundamental unit of storage, shown as either 0 or 1.
A **byte** is 8 bits.

From here you can count using the prefixes:

➤ Kilo – a kilobyte (kB) = 1000 bytes
➤ Mega – a megabyte (mB) = 1000 kB
➤ Giga – a gigabyte (gB) = 1000 mB
➤ Tera – a terabyte (tB) = 1000 gB

4-bit and 8-bit

You will remember that a bit is the smallest unit of storage: just one element – a 1 or a 0. We use these bits in bundles, or clusters, since one on its own isn't really all that useful. 4 bits are a nibble, 8 bits are a byte.

Using these combinations the computer stores all the data and presents for us on screen what we require. Graphics, sound, text and numbers must all be converted into binary for the computer to process them. They can be represented in 4- and 8-bit formats, and the basics can be shown with graphics for example:

If we code 0 as white and 1 as black, we can make this image easily with 1 bit per pixel (or square).

But black and white is limited – most graphics use more colours than this – so if we try for 2 bits per pixel we can add to this, in binary form:

1 bit per pixel: 2 possible colours
2 bits per pixel: 4 possible colours
3 bits per pixel: 8 possible colours
4 bits per pixel: 16 possible colours

So, for example:
00 stays for white
01 becomes blue
10 becomes green
11 becomes red

black 0,0,0	dark red 128,0,0	red 255,0,0	pink 255,0,255
0,128,128 teal	green 0,128,0	bright green 0,255,0	turquoise 0,255,255
dark blue 0,0,128	violet 128,0,128	blue 0,0,255	25% grey 192,192,192
50% grey 128,128,1028	dark yellow 128,0128,0	yellow 255,255,0	white 255,255,255

But this is still limited. 4-bit graphics use 4 bits per pixel, and 8 use 8 bits per pixel, to allow us to show more complex colours.

Character encoding

Since we know that computers only work in binary, we need a way of translating the **character set** (letters, numbers, and symbols) typed on the keyboard into something the computer can process. The two main methods you need to know are:

➤ **ASCII**
➤ **Unicode**

> Remember to count from the right and the letters stay the same regardless.

ASCII

ASCII stands for American Standard Code for Information Interchange. The first 32 codes (0–31) are set aside for controlling devices like printers. 32 is a space, 33 an exclamation mark, and the codes then follow the sequence along the top of a keyboard layout. There are a total of 128 characters represented by ASCII.

Unicode

Unicode is an industry standard for texts encountered in most of the world's writing systems. Unicode uses the same codes as ASCII as far as it goes – and then extends to cover a wider range of alphabets and special symbols, using between 1 and 4 bytes per character. You might have seen character coding called UTF-32, which stands for Unicode Text Formatting 32, the simplest encoding. Over 100 000 code are assigned in Unicode 6.0.

Extract from code table

ASCII/Unicode	Letter
65	A
66	B
67	C
68	D
69	E
70	F
71	G
72	H
73	I
74	J

> Once you know one code you can often work out the rest.

Both of these code the character sets in a logical pattern (such as all capital letters together, all lowercase letters together, and all letters in alphabetical order, all numbers in ascending order) so that in ASCII, 'A' is 65, and 'B' is 66, and so on.

Make coded messages with 1s and 0s that must be decoded with some squared paper. Use the ASCII table at the end of the book (or a Unicode table online) to help you design a message using the codes rather than the letters.

1. What size (in MB or GB) is the hard drive of a computer at school? Convert that number into the number of bytes. For example, a 32 MB hard drive would be 32*1024*1024 bytes – 33554432 bytes.
2. How is Unicode an improvement on ASCII?
3. If the ASCII code for 'A' is 65, what is the code for Q?

KEYWORDS

Character set ➤ The letters, numbers and symbols used on a keyboard. Different languages, and even subjects, often have different character sets

Representing images

A **pixel** is short for 'picture element', and is a single dot on your screen or printout. **Resolution** refers to how many pixels are used per square. Low resolution graphics are coarser and may seem 'furry'; high resolution graphics have more pixels per square and therefore are clearer and sharper. **Metadata** is the additional data within the graphic that identifies the date of origin, compression applied and the name of the owner of the product that created the image.

The resolution of a typical computer screen is 1920 pixels horizontally, and 1080 pixels vertically, making the number of pixels shown on the screen equal to 2 073 600 pixels.

A common graphics file type is a **bitmap**. Despite being a rather large file type because it defines *every single dot* in a graphic, this remains popular.

File name and extension	Comments
BMP	The Microsoft BMP format is barely used outside Windows: it is large and unwieldy in file size, not advised for use in web or print designs.
GIF (Graphic Image File)	This was an original format and is best used for solid colours. It is a lossless format, so even after the file has been compressed the quality remains unchanged.
JPEG (Joint Photographic Experts Group)	Possibly the most well-known format, especially on the web, also used by mobile phone and digital cameras, for example. A **JPEG** allows compression of graphics in a lossy format, meaning that quality is lost as the file is increasingly compressed, but JPEGs can also be saved in full uncompressed detail.
PNG (Portable Network Graphics)	Often used instead of one of the other two above, this can handle transparency better than a GIF format, although the files tend to come out larger.
TIFF	Another popular graphic file format, this can also be compressed to different levels. Like JPEG files they can be used uncompressed.

The size of a bitmap graphic uses pixels the same as a screen: in bits it is width (pixels) × height (pixels) × depth (bits) or in bytes (width (pixels) × height (pixels) × depth (bits))/8.

The **colour depth** of the graphic is then expressed by the number of bits used, e.g. '64-bit graphics'.

A simple 4 × 5 square shows how bitmaps are constructed:

Converting the black and white image into binary:

1	0	0	1	1	0	0	1
1	0	0	1	1	0	0	1
1	1	1	1	1	1	1	1
1	0	0	1	1	0	0	1
1	0	0	1	1	0	0	1

Common image representation

The most common way of presenting an image is called the RGB model – Red, Green, Blue. Each pixel is encoded over 32 bits (4 bytes). The fourth byte is called 'alpha' and you might have seen that in graphics work of your own. Alpha refers to the level of transparency of a graphic.

Colour	Binary (3 bytes)	Hex
White	255,255,255	FF,FF,FF
Black	0,0,0	0,0,0
Red	255,0,0	FF,0,0
Blue	0,0,255	0,0,FF
Green	0,255,0	0,FF,0
Pink	255,170,170	FF,AA,AA
Cyan	0,255,255	0,FF,FF

As a general rule, the more pixels and bits we use in a graphic, the larger the file size. Web and games designers have to consider this in their work, since if the console, phone or computer take too long to render the image, the user will go elsewhere. Compression can help with this, but the cost is often the quality of the image.

Metadata adds to the amount of information communicated with the graphic – it isn't editable so it is sometimes used to check the accuracy of other sources. It is also increasingly a privacy issue, since it can include GPS data identifying your location.

Metadata can include details such as the purpose of the file, its time and date of creation, the author or owner of the software, the location on a computer where it was stored, the standards applied to the data in the file and the file size.

Representing sound

Sound can be recorded either using digital or **analogue** equipment with analogue recording the sound waves directly onto a magnetic tape or physical record and digital taking the analogue signal and sampling it to a digital file. Many argue the quality of one is better than the other but there are many variables involved in both, from the quality of equipment used and the sampling settings used. Standard sound is 44.1 kHz – or about 44 000 samples per second.

The program takes a number of samples of the sound per second at set intervals (called the sample rate), and works out the top and bottom values of the analogue sound. If the sound being processed is above the halfway point, the program checks again if the sound would still be above halfway if the first half was cut into half again, and so on.

'Pure' sound is a perfect sine wave: this is known as the **sound wave**.

Above is recorded as a 1, below it is recorded as a 0. The number of times this is checked is reflected in the **bitrate**. These questions change the number of 'steps' that replace the smooth sine wave: again, as with graphics, the more bits the better the quality – and larger the file.

Sound file sizes are calculated based on **sampling rate** and **sample resolution**:

File size (bits) = rate × resolution × seconds

1. What are the advantages and disadvantages of using high resolution graphics on a web page?
2. Identify a situation where low resolution graphics would be an appropriate choice.

Data compression

The concept of **compression** has been mentioned in relation to graphics and sound. You need to be able to calculate the impact on file size of compression. There are two approaches to lossless data compression you need to know:

Run Length Encoding (RLE)

RLE is a very simple form of data compression which is useful when compressing graphics. 'Runs' of data with the same value are stored as a single value and count, rather than as individual values.
An example:
Coding the word FOOTBALL, this would become 1F2O1T1B1A2L. When the first digit of each pair is the frequency, and the second is the value.

The 'H' could be held, uncompressed, as 10011001111110011001

Using RLE, this can be compressed to 1 1 2 0 2 1 2 0 6 1 2 0 2 1 2 0 1 1 because the first digit of each pair is the frequency, and the second is the value.

This dark square could be held, uncompressed, as 1111 1111 1111 1111 and then becomes 16 1, which is dramatically compressed.

> This is close to the way humans compress lists: when you are ordering food with friends you might ask for two coffees, not a coffee for one person and then a coffee for the other.

Huffman coding

The more complex method used is called **Huffman coding** or **compression**, developed in 1952 by David Huffman when he was a PhD student at MIT (Massachusetts Institute of Technology). It allows for lossless compression.

Huffman coding is based on the frequency of occurrence of an element of data: the more common ones are coded with a lower number of bits so that they take up less space. Codes are stored in a code book which is created for each file. To calculate the impact on file size when data is compressed a 'Huffman tree' is created.

If you will consider the phrase 'this is an example of a Huffman tree' and work out the Huffman tree – it will look like this:

Huffman tree

Character	p	x	l	r	u	o	i	s	h	n	t	m	f	e	a	SPACE
Frequency	1	1	1	1	1	1	2	2	2	2	2	2	3	4	4	7

Table of frequency

A tree is built by working out the frequencies – in the table – and making the two lowest elements into 'leaves' creating a parent with a frequency that is the sum of the two leaves. Pulling in the other frequencies as you go, you build the tree until only one number remains.

This number is the root of your binary Huffman tree. To generate a Huffman code you go through the tree to the value you want, outputting a 0 every time you take a left-hand branch, and a 1 every time you take a right-hand branch.

Decoding a Huffman encoding is straightforward: as you read bits in from your input data you pass through the tree beginning at the root, taking the left-hand path if you read a 0 and the right-hand path if you read a 1. When you hit a leaf, you have found the code.

While ASCII is a set length (7 bits), Huffman coding is a variable length system. Calculating the size of the file depends on knowing the length of the code.

Coding the word FOOTBALL in the example below: L at 0; O at 1 (only because 0 at 0 looks odd: either way round would work) then the other letters at F = 10; T = 11; B = 100; A = 101

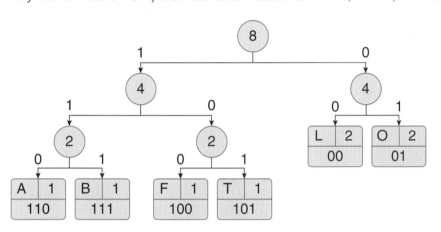

By encoding the most common letters with the smallest code, the file size can be compressed more effectively.

If data isn't compressed, then the file size is calculated remembering that each digit of an ASCII character set uses 7 bits *plus 1* because computers use 8-bit bytes.

Keeping file size small, while still holding onto as much of the original content as possible, is the dream of many designers. While we can't yet get quite that far, we can compress files as above, we can reduce the resolution or change the number of colours that are used when we save the graphic, or reduce the sample rate for sound.

Range of options available for saving file

1. a) Use Huffman coding to work out the compressed size of your name.
    b) Compare that to the size of your name in ASCII. Which is the better choice?

Fundamentals of data representation

Number bases

Decimal
- Base 10
- Most familiar to us!

Hexadecimal
- Base 16
- Goes from 0–9 then A–F
- Most user-friendly way of representing binary as a 4-bit (nibble)

Binary
- Base 2
- Closest to the way the computer works
- Only shows 1 and 0 (on and off)

Data compression

RLE (Run length encoding)
- Encodes the 'runs' of identical value and their frequencies

Huffman coding
- Work out the frequencies to form a tree

Encoding

Character sets
- All keys on a keyboard
- Differ depending on language and sometimes purpose

Main types
- ASCII – English language characters
- Unicode – Covers most languages in the world – Extends ASCII

Graphics
- More bits per pixel = more colours

Units

Bit – fundamental unit of storage

Byte – 8 bits

Prefixes
- Kilobyte = 1000 bytes
- Megabyte = 1000 kilobytes
- Gigabyte = 1000 megabytes
- Terrabyte = 1000 gigabytes

Arithmetic

Binary shift
- Worth knowing about carry over numbers, but not essential!

Arithmetic shift left
- Multiply by 2

Arithmetic shift right
- Divide by 2

Logical shift left
- Insert 0 to the right, lose the leftmost digit

Logical shift right
- Insert to the left, lose the rightmost digit

If you need more space to answer the following questions, please use a separate piece of paper.

1. Convert 10111110 from binary into decimal. **(1 mark)**

_____

2. Calculate 15 – 14 in hexadecimal. Give your answer in hexadecimal. **(1 mark)**

_____

3. Calculate 20 – 8 in hexadecimal. Give your answer in hexadecimal. **(1 mark)**

_____

4. Calculate 20 – 8 in binary. Give your answer in hexadecimal. **(1 mark)**

_____

5. Convert 3F from hexadecimal into decimal. **(1 mark)**

_____

6. Convert 60 from hexadecimal into binary. **(1 mark)**

_____

7. Convert 101 from binary into hexadecimal. **(1 mark)**

_____

8. The ASCII character set uses 7 bits to encode every character.
   Why is there a different code for uppercase and lowercase letters? **(3 marks)**

_____

_____

9. How would this be coded in 1-bit colour? **(3 marks)**

_____

_____

_____

10. How many possible colours may be coded with 4 bits per pixel? **(1 mark)**

_____

11. Explain how sound is encoded so that it can be transferred from natural
    analogue to digital files. **(5 marks)**

_____

_____

_____

_____

_____

Hardware and software

In essence, a computer is the product of **hardware** and **software**. It is no use having the newest and fastest computer if it has no programs, and the best software in the world cannot operate without hardware of some sort.

Hardware refers to the parts of the computer that can be touched or seen: they are the physical components – they're 'hard'. Software is the coding, from the machine code to the top level language, which makes the computer perform the operations required.

Hardware

Software

Boolean logic and truth tables

20

You ought to remember the word 'Boolean' from Internet searches, but it originally refers to the construction of 'logic gates' in computer science. We use **truth tables** to show how each gate works.

There are only three gates that you need to know well:

1. AND gates
2. NOT gates
3. OR gates

 These may be familiar from circuit work in Technology or Science.

AND gates

An AND gate requires the two inputs to be '1' or 'on' before it will operate. In human terms, that could be 'weekday' AND 'school day' = 'wear uniform', or a light will only turn on if two switches are pressed.

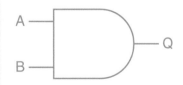

The truth table for an AND gate looks like this, and you can see that it only turns 'on' when both of the inputs are also 'on'.

A	B	Q
0	0	0
0	1	0
1	0	0
1	1	1

NOT gates

A NOT gate has a single input and the output of the circuit will be the opposite of the input.

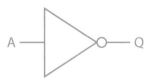

The truth table for a NOT gate looks like this:

A	Q
1	0
0	1

OR gates

The last gate you need to learn is an OR gate, and the meaning of this one is clear from its name: an OR gate operates when either of the inputs is '1' or 'on'.

The truth table for an OR gate looks like this:

A	B	Q
0	0	0
0	1	1
1	0	1
1	1	1

The examples shown in all cases have two inputs – but the rules still work with three or more. An AND gate requires them all to be '1' or 'on', a NOT looks for inputs that show '0' or 'off' and an OR will take the '1' or 'on' signal from any of the inputs.

Combining logic gates

Logic gates can be combined.

An AND gate followed by a NOT gate would look like this:

To work this out you would need to follow the data, so start with the AND gate:

A	B	C
0	0	0
0	1	0
1	0	0
1	1	1

Then send the C input into the NOT gate to find Q:

A	B	C	Q
0	0	0	1
0	1	0	1
1	0	0	1
1	1	1	0

This can also be written in text form as Q = NOT (A AND B) because Q is the NOT output from the AND of A and B.

Design an interactive poster with pockets that you can fill with counters to show each of the gates in action.

1. If a gate has two inputs and operates when either input is on, which type of gate is it?
2. If a gate has four inputs and only operates when all four are on, which type of gate is it?

Classification

There are two main types of software that you need to be able to distinguish:

1. System software, including **operating systems** and utility programs
2. Application software

System software

System software is the software that operates the computer hardware itself – not anything that you interact with, except possibly to log in, or respond to messages. Within this definition are operating systems, device drivers, virus protection programs and computer maintenance programs such as disk defragmenters.

Without system software, computers of all types simply wouldn't operate at all. All other software runs through the system software.

Operating systems

Operating systems (OS) are key to the function of any computer.

➤ The OS controls the operation of the processor and memory, by managing the resources so that each application is allocated enough processor time and power, memory and hard drive space to complete its job. In this, the OS is like a referee, making sure everyone plays a fair game.

➤ The OS controls any peripherals, like printers, scanners, barcode readers that are attached to the computer. It will use specialised drivers to ensure that the right instructions are passed in a way that the device can operate.

➤ The OS controls security – logins and sometimes basic firewalls and anti-virus facilities are run through the OS.

➤ The OS provides a foundation for all application software to run, allowing software developers to write for an operating system rather than for a computer design, as was the case in the early years of computer development. This is because each OS has a standardised API (application program interface).

There are many different types of OS – Android, Windows X and Mac OSX are probably familiar to you, but there are others such as UNIX and different types of LINUX like Debian and Mint. Some are proprietary, which usually means you pay for them, while the LINUX types are all 'free'.

Utility programs

Utility programs perform specialised tasks, rather than juggle lots of demands like the OS. Some utility programs are included in the OS, such as disk defragmenting and file compression. Anti-virus (AV) and firewall programs may be utility programs with which you are already familiar. Regularly updated security software is essential for safe function online.

Application software

Application software is the software that you as the user install, and it is the software with which you work most frequently. Word processing or presentation or spreadsheet software is application software, as are your email client and Internet browser. Again, as with utility software, application software tends to be installed for a specific purpose, such as managing emails or browsing the Internet.

> Be careful not to use brand names when referring to software.

KEYWORDS

Operating systems ➤ Platforms on which all other programs run. They manage input to and output from the processing unit

Utility programs ➤ Written to complete one task, such as cleaning your operating system registry, or testing your RAM to ensure it is still functioning

Application software ➤ Software that the user installs to perform defined tasks

1. Why is it important to use anti-virus and firewall software if you want to spend time online?
2. Identify two different operating systems and compare their benefits and drawbacks.
3. Identify the function of utility programs.
4. What function does the operating system perform?

Use colour-coded cards to identify each 'layer' of software in a system. Stack them up so you have a clear image of how they work together.

Von Neumann

The traditional computer architecture we all recognise is Von Neumann architecture, or Von Neumann concept.

You need to remember that this really only applies to the **stored-program** computers, in which an 'instruction fetch' and 'data operation' cannot occur at the same time because they use the same **bus**. This is called the 'Von Neumann bottleneck'.

Traffic along a bus in the model shown can only go one way at a time – it is a serial connection – and therefore the performance of the computer was significantly slowed.

Modern architecture overcomes this because the same memory is used for both program instructions and data.

The **fetch-execute cycle** is the process by which the CPU reads (fetches) instructions from the memory cache, decodes them, and then operates – or executes – the instruction.

Components

Memory
Memory is generally categorised as **ROM** (Read Only Memory) and **RAM** (Random Access Memory).
➤ Read Only Memory provides the computer with instructions that do not change – such as boot setup.
➤ Random Access Memory is the working space in which the computer stores data in current use. This is **volatile** because once the power is switched off the data is lost.

There are different levels of memory, including cache memory and registers, which are on the CPU rather than in separate places on the circuit board, where the main memory chip connectors are located.

The computer uses cache memory as a form of buffer because the CPU works faster than RAM. The data is pushed into cache memory before the CPU needs it to stop the slower memory inhibiting the function of the CPU. Cache memory also stores frequently used instructions so the processor can access them faster than from RAM each time.

A register is a small amount of storage not accessed by **main memory** and is the fastest way to get data to the CPU. Data used most frequently can be stored in registers to ensure the fastest access time.

Processor

The speed of a computer processor is often referred to as **clock speed**. This refers to the internal clock in the CPU that keeps everything working to time, like a conductor keeps an orchestra synchronised. The faster the clock, the more instructions a CPU can execute per second.

Clock speeds are measured in MHz (megahertz) or GHz (gigahertz). One megahertz equals one million cycles per second – but remember that a 2 GHz CPU is not necessarily double the speed of a 1GHz CPU because the memory, the task and the number of **cores** will all make a difference. **Clock-digital circuits** use a clock signal to ensure all parts of the circuit remain synchronised. On a modern processor chip, this is essential due to the high speed of processing.

Buses

Buses are pathways around the motherboard that connect the components that are attached. There are two main types of 'buses' in a computer: the internal bus carries data within the motherboard, and the external bus communicates data with peripherals and devices attached to the motherboard.

Each bus has pins or lines – there are three types:
- Control – used to send out messages to co-ordinate the activities on the motherboard
- Address – used to pass memory addresses from one component to another
- Data – transfers the data between all components.

The processor bus you may have already heard of, called the FSB or Front-Side Bus, carried data between the CPU and the memory controller, called northbridge by IBM, in the 1990s.

ALU

The **ALU** (Arithmetic-Logic Unit) performs the mathematical and logical operations required by the code, and then passes the result to the memory. Therefore, it does the mathematics (1 + 2 = 3) and the logic (Is this string longer than that?).

1. Explain why a 1GHz CPU might not be half as fast as a 2GHz CPU.
2. Describe the Von Neumann bottleneck.
3. What are the main limits of the Von Neumann model?

Secondary storage

Any storage that is outside the CPU – such as hard drives, DVD drives, USB and other solid state storage – is referred to as secondary storage. It is large enough to store the programs we want to run, and is **non-volatile** so the data remains after the power is switched off. If we relied on RAM for all of our memory needs, we would have to install programs every time we wanted to use them, and the programs would have to be much smaller and less powerful.

As files have increased in size, and people have wanted to store more and more data, **cloud storage** has become popular. **Cloud computing** is the term for processing your data on computer systems belonging to someone else, and accessing them through the Internet. Storage companies use ranks of data servers in stacks, using either large traditional magnetic hard drives or, increasingly as capacity expands, solid state drives. This has a number of implications:

Advantages of cloud storage	Disadvantages of cloud storage
Access from anywhere with Internet connection.	You need a reliable Internet connection – especially if you are handling large files.
For businesses, this means that offices across the world can access the same files.	You are relying on someone else to keep your files safe.
Disaster recovery is easier – assuming that your storage provider wasn't affected by whatever hit your system.	Moving from one provider to another can be difficult.
Costs are generally lower per mB and storage capacity is more flexible than local storage.	There can be data ownership issues if your provider is sold to another company – when Facebook bought Instagram, all Instagram content transferred a 'license to use' that content to Facebook – without the users' express consent.

The other option is to store your files locally. This can be either truly local – attached to your computer through an internal or external port – or networked. Network Attached Storage is a term that refers to hard drives attached to a network of computers solely for the purposes of storage. You access them usually through mapping a drive letter, like N:\ or S:\ for example, and the array of disks is treated as if it is one large hard drive.

Advantages of local storage	Disadvantages of local storage
You have control of your data	The capacity is limited by the drive space and your budget.
No Internet connection required – you have direct access.	Not always convenient to access.
Saving data is faster than cloud storage.	Possibility of theft.
External drives are cheap and have considerable capacity for the non-specialist to use to extend their data storage.	Data recovery in event of a disaster is down to the user.

Computer architecture is also found in **embedded systems**, such as digital watches, MP3 players, MRI scanners and traffic lights. An embedded system is one in which the computer system plays a part in a much bigger device. The computer element is often nearly invisible, but essential. Unlike non-embedded systems, embedded systems are generally designed to perform a single task rather than be general purpose computers.

	Operation	Advantages	Disadvantages
Solid state drive (SSD)	SSDs use a grid of electrical cells to quickly send and receive data. These grids are separated into sections called 'pages' and these pages are where the data is stored. Pages are clumped together to form "blocks". SSDs can only write to blank pages in the blocks, and only delete pages when there isn't enough space left to store the data required. As a result SSDs perform less and less well over time.	The only drives currently available that are faster than hard drives (magnetic). Start up faster since there are no moving parts. Some are waterproof. Ideal for portable USB devices.	Very expensive compared to other forms of storage. Limited write cycles – these wear out much faster than anything else. Write speeds can be slow.
Optical **(CD/DVD/ Blu-ray)**	A CD/DVD/Blu-ray has a single track of data spiralling from the centre to the edge of the disk. These are made up of bumps on one side, which show up as microscopic pits on the other. The drive motor moves a laser and lens system to exactly focus on the area to be read/written. The bumps (or pits) reflect the laser differently from the flat 'lands' in between, and the electronics in the drive interpret this to read the data.	Portable. On some formats, data can be archived because it cannot be over-written (DVD-R/CD-R). Inexpensive.	Require special drives to write to them. Relatively small capacity. Easily damaged. Some compatibility issues across drives.
Magnetic (hard disk drive-HDD)	Hard drives contain spinning platters which are accessed by a read/write head on an arm. This can move from the centre to the edge of the platter up to 50 times per second. Data is stored in sectors and tracks – a track is one circle around the disk, a sector is a section of the arc. The operating system often organises sectors into clusters.	One of the cheapest methods to store data. Fast access to data. Direct access to any part of the drive.	The disks eventually fail. Surface can become damaged leading to data corruption. Cannot easily transfer between computers.

KEYWORDS

Cloud computing ➤ Rather than relying on the local processing power of a single computer, cloud computing allows the processing of data on a network or Internet connected remote system. This can also be extended to storage

23

 Investigate the storage capacities and prices of CD/DVD/Blu-ray disks. How do they compare to portable USB devices for example?

1. If I want to store my personal data, would you recommend that I use cloud or local storage? Why?
2. If volatile memory loses all its contents whenever the power is switched off, why do we use it?

Computer systems

Systems architecture

CPU
- ALU
- Control unit

Von Neumann
- Bottleneck

Fetch – execute process

Memory
- Volatile (e.g. RAM) – cache and register
- Non-volatile (e.g. ROM)

Clock and clock speed
- Measured in MHz and GHz

Secondary storage
- Local – hard drives, DVD, SSD
- Cloud

Cores

System
- Computer = hardware + software
- Doesn't have to look like a computer!

System software

Operating systems
- Proprietary – Windows and Mac OSX
- Free – LINUX types
- Function – manage the hardware

Utility programs
- Generally single task – anti-virus, file compression

Device drivers
- Specific to each device: allows communication between processor and device

Application software
- Word processing and 'office functions'
- Bought for specific purpose
  - Email
  - Internet browser
  - Games

Logic gates
- AND
- NOT
- OR

If you need more space to answer the following questions, please use a separate piece of paper.

1. A modern smartphone allows the user to input data through the use of a touch screen. State three other ways in which data can be input to a smartphone. **(3 marks)**

_____

_____

_____

2. Smartphones use solid state media rather than magnetic storage. Identify two differences between these types of storage media and suggest why smartphones use solid state storage. **(3 marks)**

_____

_____

_____

3. The output of an AND gate with three inputs (A,B,C) is ON when any one input is ON. State whether this is true or false. **(1 mark)**

_____

4. What would be the output of this combination of logic gates if A is ON and B is OFF? **(2 marks)**

_____

_____

_____

5. Describe the Von Neumann model of computer architecture. **(5 marks)**

_____

_____

_____

_____

6. What is the fetch-execute cycle? **(3 marks)**

_____

_____

7. Why is it important for computers to have adequate capacity of RAM? **(2 marks)**

_____

_____

8. A lot of companies are now using 'the cloud' for data storage. What is 'the cloud' and why are companies moving their data into this form of storage? **(3 marks)**

_____

_____

_____

Definitions and types

A network is a computer system comprising linked elements such as computers, file storage and printers. Most networks share the attribute that users must log on, though some are 'distributed' so that the user has no idea of the construction of the network or of other devices in it.

There are a variety of different types of network within that definition that you need to know:

Local Area Network (**LAN**): A network in which all connected devices are relatively close together, in a single building or premises, like a school or office complex. Because the distances involved are fairly short, cables can be used to establish physical links between each device and the servers and resources, usually through switches. Wireless and fibre optic connections also suit this type of network. LANs usually operate within single organisations.

Wide Area Network (**WAN**): A network in which the connected devices are too thinly spread to make a physical connection. These tend to be connected through telephone lines, undersea cables and, in extreme cases, satellite links. In a multinational organisation, there may be LANs within cities, and a WAN linking all the LANs into one large web. At the most extreme, the Internet could be seen as a WAN. Sometimes, as in the case of the Net, elements of a WAN are owned by different people or organisations.

Different components of a LAN

Arguably, the largest WAN is the Internet itself

Personal Area Network (PAN): A network often based on Bluetooth connection between devices such as keyboards, pointing devices, phones, audio headsets and printers. These cover very short distances (up to about 10 metres) but have the advantage that they can move with the user.

Wired or wireless: wired networks can use copper 'Cat5' ethernet cable for short distance connectivity (up to about 100 m from device to switch), with fibre optic cable used for longer distances. Wireless networks remove the need for cables but all devices on the network require connectivity.

	Advantages	Disadvantages
Wired network	Reliable connection. Usually faster than wireless connections. More secure.	Not portable – you're tied to the workspace. Generally more expensive to set up because every device needs a separate cable.
Wireless network	Portable. Can easily add and remove devices.	Can lose signal under less than ideal conditions. Security can be an issue if passwords and other settings aren't strong. Can be slow – especially if the access point (WAP) is shared between devices.

KEYWORDS

LAN ➤ Local Area Network. A network for one organisation, usually on one site, or sites which are geographically close

WAN ➤ Wide Area Network. A network usually for one organisation, covering a much wider area, often countries or continents

Investigate the most common wireless security protocols-WEP, WPA and WPA2-and produce a factsheet on why they are important.

1. When designing a new network for a school, which structure would you recommend, and why?
2. Would a travelling DJ be better off investing in wired or wireless kit? Why?

Topology

There are four main types of topology (or shape) that you need to know:

Topology	Description	Advantages	Disadvantages
Star	The star topology is probably the most expensive: it is also the fastest. Each device has its own connection to the server, which means that a lot of cabling can be needed.	Most reliable design: any single failure is local and doesn't affect the rest of the network (unless it's the server that fails). Simple to troubleshoot because failures are localised. Adding devices doesn't affect speed of performance until server capacity is reached. Easy to upgrade or expand elements independently. **Best used in a larger organisation than a household if only because of the expense.**	Uses more cable than any other design. Uses additional hardware (routers/switches/hubs) which adds again to the cost. If the switch fails, the whole element of the network supported by it crashes. If the server goes down, the whole network collapses. Can require more technical know-how to set up.
Bus	A bus network has a central spine of network cabling, called a bus (remember this from the Von Neumann architecture?), which transports the signals.	Simple and cheapest to install. Good for a temporary network. Flexible because elements can be removed or added without messing with the rest of the network. **Best used in small or temporary networks – can be a useful home network solution.**	If the bus (spine) fails, the whole network crashes. Performance is affected by load – the more devices attached, the slower it functions. Bus cables are limited in length and must be terminated properly to avoid reflection of signal, which can crash the system. Data has to 'queue' sometimes because the bus is busy with other demands.
Ring	A ring network has all of the computers connected to each other in a circle.	Data can be transmitted from different devices simultaneously, making communication more reliable and faster. This can handle high levels of traffic because each device shares the load. Expansion is easy without unsettling anything already installed. Ideal for wireless connections.	Expensive to cable. High levels of redundancy question the cost effectiveness in this model. Setup and maintenance is difficult. Administration of all nodes can be complex.
Mesh	A mesh network interconnects each device with all of the others, sharing the load for data communication, and generally producing a much more reliable function.	Fast data flow when it is working well – all data flows in one direction. Even when the load is the same, this performs better than a bus setup. Each device can access the resources on the network equally.	Each packet of data has to travel through all of the devices between its origin and its destination. If one device malfunctions the whole network is compromised. Setting this up is more expensive than a bus network.

Network security

Any network requires security settings. Stories on the news almost every week highlight what happens when security is breached and data released or destroyed. When you run a network holding the data for the organisation or personal data of clients and employees, the responsibility to maintain security is considerable. If your network is holding personal data, your responsibility is also identified in legislation like the Data Protection Act. The Information Commissioner is responsible for investigating breaches of data security where there is a question of negligence.

The main methods of network security that you need to know are:

Authentication: Checking the identity of a user, often by checking their user name exists, and that their password matches. Obviously this is vulnerable to hacking, and passwords should be changed regularly and frequently, meeting high standards of robustness.

Encryption: Makes data appear meaningless and provides security for the content both when stored electronically and when transmitted using an encryption key. **Decryption** uses the decryption key to convert the data back to an intelligible form.

Firewall: A software or hardware product used in a network to prevent external users gaining unauthorised access to a computer system. Firewalls limit the data and instructions that are transferred to a server, sometimes by blocking a specific **port** on the computers, sometimes by requiring that the transmitting device be on a **whitelist** of authorised devices. The port is the visible connection to channels on the motherboard that transfer data.

MAC address filtering: Using a **MAC address**, a whitelist of authorised devices can be maintained and any unknown devices questioned or blocked.

Whitelist: Identifies authorised sites if on an Internet filter, or users or machines if on a firewall. Only those on the whitelist are allowed through.

Blacklist: Bars only those devices or addresses identified on the blacklist.

Most networks will run all of these systems to help ensure that only authorised users and devices access network resources.

KEYWORDS

Port ➤ Identifies where a channel enters or leaves a computer system: this is a physical location where components can be plugged into the device. Ports are often given port numbers to enable easy selection and identification

Whitelist ➤ Identifies authorised sites if on an Internet filter, or users or machines if on a firewall. Only those on the whitelist are allowed through. This is more secure than the blacklist because that simply bars only those identified on the list: the whitelist bars everything except what is on the list

MAC address ➤ Short for Media Access Control address, a MAC address is inbuilt in the hardware for any device that may need to connect to a network

Use match boxes and string to create models of the different topologies.

1. A small company in one building has five computers: they want to network them but have very little money. Which type of topology would you recommend and why?
2. There are two controls – whitelist and blacklist. Which is the stronger setup and why?

Network protocols

Devices on any network from a home to the Internet must follow **protocols** if they are to communicate and function effectively on that network. The ones you must know are:

Protocols	Description
Ethernet	This protocol comprises a number of components and standards. It is made up of the frames in which the data is sent around the network; the *physical layer*, which is the actual transmission of the signal including the clock signal to ensure the sending and receiving clocks are in sync, and the MAC address, which identifies the sending device. To send data, the device first listens to check whether the connection is free. If it is busy it waits for a set delay and checks again until it can send the data.
Wi-Fi	This is in reality a range of different protocols rather than one. Wi-Fi is a trademark. The correct term for wireless networks is **WLAN** and they are identified by the number 802.11 with a letter following it to identify its generation. The fastest currently is 802.11ac, which has a maximum data rate of 1.3 Gbps.
TCP	This stands for Transmission Control Protocol, and is a standard that defines how to establish and maintain a link through with programs can transmit and receive data. You might have come across it in connection with TCP/IP. TCP controls how each message is broken into **packets** that the network can transport, checks that all the packets have reached their destination (and re-sends those that are lost), and receives packets in turn from the **network layer**. All communication is sent in packets to balance the load, whether that be in a two-device home network or the Internet. Packets have headers, which are like envelopes showing the destination address.
IP	Internet Protocol is the main communications protocol. This works with TCP to address data packets accurately and decides the best route to use to send the data. Some data packets will take different routes to reach the same destination if the network is particularly busy and it is quicker to send some data 'around' the bottleneck.
HTTP(s)	This stands for HyperText Transfer Protocol, and the additional 's' is the more secure method of transmission. This runs on a **client-server** architecture, and examples of a server include Apache Web Server and Internet Information Server (IIS). The client is also called a Web browser, and examples include Firefox, Chrome, Edge and Safari.
SMTP	Simple Mail Transfer Protocol also operates on the client-server model. The sending email program contacts the mail server of the destination to indicate that a message is coming, and waits for a 'ready' message in return. The message is then sent in stages, with the receiving server confirming each one, rather like you repeating a message that someone tells you in a telephone conversation.
IMAP	Internet Message Access Protocol differs from SMTP in that when you use IMAP you leave a copy of the message on the email server, rather than downloading it to your device. This has the advantage that you can access your email messages from anywhere with a signal, but it does make management and security of messages more complex.
FTP	File Transfer Protocol uses the client-server architecture to connect devices, often using a login and password to confirm secure transmission. FTP is less common now as a separate technology, though it is incorporated into many web page editing software packages.
UDP	User Datagram Protocol isn't as reliable as TCP but is much simpler and is useful for a less specific broadcast type of task rather than communication to a specific recipient. It doesn't check for errors in broadcast, or resend lost data packets, so it is faster than TCP.
POP3	Post Office Protocol 3 is used to log into and retrieve messages from an email server and download it to your computer or device. Most email clients using this protocol periodically check for new messages and once downloaded, messages are normally deleted from the server.

TCP/IP

This is such a significant part of the operation of the Internet that you need to know more about this separately from the other protocols. The TCP/IP model of the Internet looks like this:

| APPLICATION LAYER | ← | The topmost layer includes protocols like **DNS**, HTTP(s), SMTP, IMAP, **SSH**, FTP. This controls how applications access data and communicate. |

| TRANSPORT LAYER | ← | The Transport Layer sits beneath the application layer and permits devices on at each end of a connection to have a conversation. This operates TCP and UDP. |

26

| INTERNET LAYER | ← | The Internet Layer is second from bottom. It packs data into packets that include the source and destination addresses and the order in which the higher layers should reassemble the packets on arrival. |

| NETWORK ACCESS (or DATA LINK) LAYER | ← | The Network Access Layer defines how data is physically sent through the network, controlling the hardware along the route. Protocols in operation here include IP and Ethernet. You can see evidence of the layer when you view the NIC (Network Interface Card) in your computer. |

In the Application Layer you will find the programs, or applications, such as email and web browsers. They are at the top because they do not hold the details of connectivity – like drivers don't control how the roads are constructed or the traffic lights.

The Transport Layer sets up the communication between the sender and the destination, making sure they agree the 'language' and also that the recipient knows the size and number of packets that it should expect. If any go astray the Transport Layer automatically tries a number of times to re-send before transmitting a 'failed' message to the original sender so that they know the message went astray.

Make a model of the TCP/IP layer and add sticky notes to show which protocols operate where: use colour codes. Then ask a friend to remove one and see if you can work out which is missing.

1. What does FTP stand for?
2. True or false – The Internet Protocol (IP) is the foundation layer of the Internet.
3. What is the difference between IMAP and SMTP?

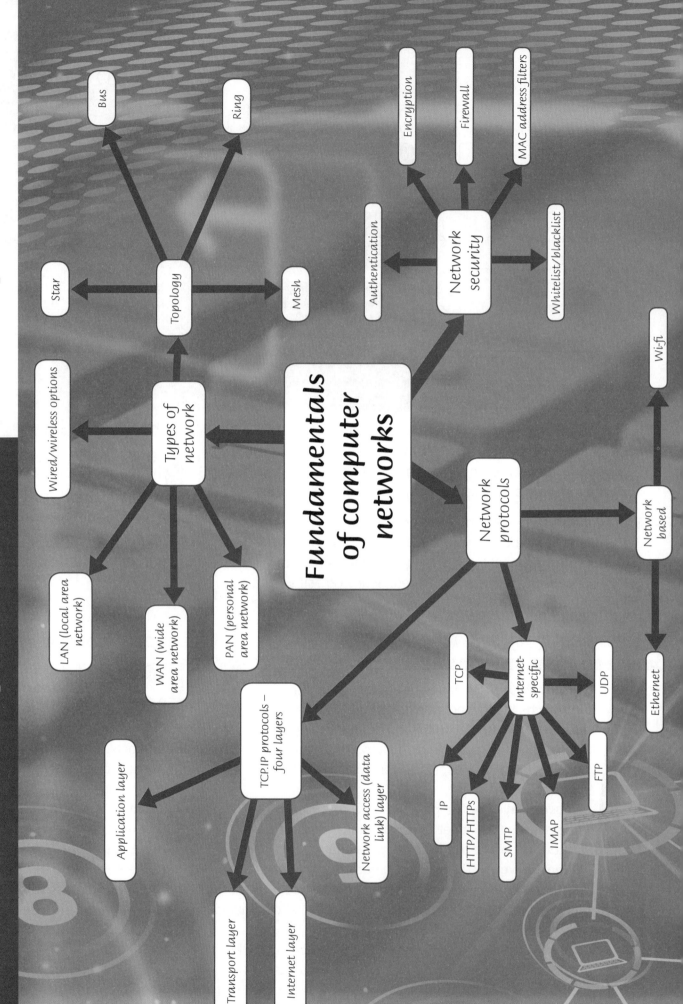

Fundamentals of computer networks

Types of network
- Wired/wireless options
- Topology
  - Star
  - Bus
  - Ring
  - Mesh
- LAN (local area network)
- WAN (wide area network)
- PAN (personal area network)

Network security
- Encryption
- Firewall
- MAC address filters
- Authentication
- Whitelist/blacklist

Network protocols
- TCP.IP protocols – four layers
  - Application layer
  - Transport layer
  - Internet layer
  - Network access (data link) layer
- Internet-specific
  - TCP
  - UDP
  - IP
  - HTTP/HTTPs
  - SMTP
  - IMAP
  - FTP
- Network based
  - Wi-fi
  - Ethernet

If you need more space to answer the following questions, please use a separate piece of paper.

1. A friend is setting up their home network and Internet access with two computers, three tablets and their phone. Would you recommend that they use wired or wireless? Give two reasons in your answer. **(3 marks)**

_____

_____

2. When would bus topology be a useful structure for network design? **(2 marks)**

_____

3. How does encryption aid security on a network? **(2 marks)**

_____

4. What is the difference between a whitelist and a blacklist? Explain which is the more secure. **(4 marks)**

_____

_____

5. What is the client-server model? **(2 marks)**

_____

6. What type of network is the Internet? **(1 mark)**

_____

7. Identify each of the layers of the TCP/IP model of the Internet. **(4 marks)**

┌─────────────────────┐
│   │
│   │
└─────────────────────┘

┌─────────────────────┐
│   │
│   │
└─────────────────────┘

┌─────────────────────┐
│   │
│   │
└─────────────────────┘

┌─────────────────────┐
│   │
│   │
└─────────────────────┘

8. What topology is shown in this diagram? **(1 mark)**

_____

Definition and purpose

Cyber security refers to the range of strategies we use to protect computers, programs and data from malicious attack or damage.

There are an increasing number of styles and types of attack, and it is worth reading technology and business news headlines to be aware of up to date information.

Types of threat

The main cyber security threats that you need to know about are:

Threat	Description
Malicious code	Any element of code in a software system that is designed to breach security or damage the system, including **viruses**, **worms**, logic bombs, **Trojan horses** (**backdoor** and trapdoor) and other **malware**. **Spyware** is the generic term for programs like **keyloggers** that hunt out and transmit to a third party details held on computer systems. Your best defence here is common sense and caution, supported by up-to-date anti-virus and firewall provision.
Poor password practice	Many hackers rely on users failing to recognise the important of strong passwords and exploiting the following examples of poor practice: • Leaving any device, website or software password at its default admin setting. • Using the same password for many services: a social network and bank account for example. • Using one of the many commonly-held passwords: p@55w0rd, for example.
Poor access rights configuration/Network policy weaknesses	Keeping track of who can access what is essential for any computer system, including deleting the user privileges of those who leave the organisation. A good network policy includes the ways in which this can be done – allowing no other, so that standardised approaches are used across the organisation. It also specifies the computer systems themselves, so that software and hardware are all to the same minimum specification, and sets up a regular audit of all procedures, to ensure the rules are being followed.
Unpatched and/or outdated software	Browser and operating system, driver and application software, are regularly updated to ensure robustness and security – and malware writers are constantly benefitting from those who delay their updating.
Removable media	The growing availability and capacity of removable media such as USB storage devices and Bluetooth connected devices means that your computer can be infected without ever connecting to the Internet. Malware, viruses or other executable programs can be transferred to a device disguised as a user-friendly file and then run accidentally at any time.
Brute force attack	A brute force attack goes through every possible combination of passwords. This could take days or more depending on the strength of the encryption, the strength of the password and any other protective measures taken.
Distributed denial of service (DDOS)	This is when a site is attacked by a number of systems, causing the server to shut down access to legitimate users or even to entirely shut down. The attacker compromises one computer and takes over its access to the Internet, then uses it to infect others with malware that allows them to be controlled. A computer under such control is known as a 'zombie' or 'bot', and botnets (collections of these hijacked computers) are considered one of the biggest current threats to Internet security.

SQL injection	This involves targeting database-based websites, such as an online retailer, and inserting malicious SQL statements into the website database server that has a weakness or vulnerability. Attackers may then be able to spoof their identity, edit financial or personal information or simply delete important data.
Ransomware	Ransomware is a type of malware that infects a computer system in some way and the user is asked to pay a fee, or ransom, to remove the malware and free their system.
Social engineering techniques	Social engineering attempts to trick a user into revealing security information through ruses such as pretending to be a new employee, or a colleague from another branch, or someone begging you for help. Asking them to contact you back on an organisation phone extension can be one method of defence, since email addresses can easily be faked. Types of social engineering include: ➤ Blagging: creating and using a fake story to fool a victim to reveal secure information that they would otherwise keep secret. ➤ Phishing: fraudulently obtaining information by claiming to be a reputable organisation, such as pretending to be a bank requesting login details. This is often done using email or text message. Sometimes referred to as 'smishing'. ➤ Pharming: an attack against a website, directing legitimate traffic to a fake site. This is why it is best to use your own bookmarks/favourites rather than rely on a typed-in web address. Attacks are not only virtual – 'shouldering' is when you watch someone type in their PIN at a cash machine (ATM) or in a store and then snatch their card.
Adware	This is justified as a way of paying for software for which the user might not want to pay in money. Advertisements are included in the software program and are displayed at intervals during use.

KEYWORDS

Virus ➤ A program which has been written to replicate itself on the host computer and across to other unprotected computers where it has access

Worm ➤ A program that spreads itself through network connections to other systems

Trojan horse ➤ A program that appears to be benign but is actually causing damage that the user often cannot see until it is too late

Backdoor Trojan ➤ Also known as Trapdoor Trojan, is a program left by a hacker allowing free unauthorised access to otherwise secured elements of a computer system

Malware ➤ Generic term for software that users may unwittingly download onto their computers, ranging from viruses to keyloggers and spyware

Spyware ➤ Spyware is the generic term for programs like keyloggers that hunt out and transmit to a third party details held on computer systems

Keylogger ➤ Records all typing on the keyboard, and transmit this to its owner. This can clearly include passwords and other identity information

1. How can a program stored on a USB storage device be considered a threat to a computer system?
2. Does a computer system not attached to the Internet need a firewall? Why?
3. How does a phishing email try to gain information from you?

Defence against cyber security threats

The weakest link in any computer system is the user, and a number of strategies have been developed to try to strengthen this element.

The main cyber security defence elements that you need to know about are:

	Best suited to	Strengths	Weaknesses
Biometric measures (fingerprints, eye scans, hand or palm geometry, typing patterns, facial recognition)	Mobile devices, especially fingerprint Other devices with peripherals for **biometrics**	High level of accuracy. Most cost-effective form of biometrics currently available is fingerprint, which is also the most common. Eye and facial scans are loved in movies but this is expensive tech. Signature, voice and typing recognition look for similarity to stored patterns rather than understanding the phrase, 'open sesame!' Easy to use. Non-intrusive. Small storage requirements on the system for fingerprint.	Some people find it uncomfortable since it is linked to criminal identification. Can make mistakes. Not ideal for children since, for example, their fingerprints are still growing.
Password systems	Any device	Cheapest security system of all. If frequently changed, passwords can be among the most secure access devices. No specialist hardware required.	People forget them! Vulnerable to brute force attacks and keyloggers. Depend on users using a secure combination – and only once for each login.
CAPTCHA (or a simple tick box stating 'I am not a robot')	Online resources	Distinguishes between human access attempt and machine brute force attempt. Limits spamming and bot attacks. Audio version offered. Hard-to-impossible for optical character recognition to read.	Can be difficult to read – especially for people with visual impairments. Some browsers don't render them accurately. Audio version isn't always clear enough to understand. Requires a keyboard so not entirely user friendly.
Email confirmations	Online resources	If password is encrypted, then the only information passed is a link to reset the original password, so resources stay secure. Depends on accurate setup and correct email address typed in.	Can be delayed or caught by spam/junk mail filters. If password not encrypted, and that is sent by open email there is clear risk of abuse. If you mistype your email address the message goes astray.

Detecting and preventing threats

Module 28

Automatic software updates	Local installation of online copies – drivers, operating systems, application programs	Avoids the 'user problem' altogether. Keeps software up to date selecting the right elements each time.	Some feel this is an invasion of privacy. Requires that the computer system is operating at pre-arranged times. Can slow Internet access speeds.

Others include:

Access levels

An option often overlooked, this can limit the opportunity for someone to wittingly or unwittingly cause damage across a network. Network users are assigned a level of control over resources on the network that match their role and no more. In a school, only the network manager and possibly the head teacher will have 'total' control: others will have progressively less control since they don't need it. On the odd occasion when someone needs a task completed they would need to ask someone who has the level of access necessary. This adds a level of checking as well as a trail of action.

Firewall

A firewall is a system – hardware- or software-based – which scrutinises network traffic and applies a set of rules to limit the possibility of illegitimate traffic passing through. This is a barrier between 'trusted' devices on the same network and less trusted devices or networks – such as the Internet. Some organisations take this further by including a proxy server, which is an additional intermediary between the trusted and the not-trusted devices.

Anti-virus software

This now often includes protection against a range of malware, and adds a layer of protection against malicious software. The simplest kinds rely on scans to check through your hard drive, while others are constantly actively scanning for changes in your data that could be caused by malicious software. It must be said that all AV/firewall software is only as good as the operator, and nothing can override your choosing 'yes' to install something nasty.

Encryption

This is the conversion of an original message (plaintext) into a code (ciphertext) using a key. Encryption is now essential to much communication over the Internet: secure e-commerce, banking and other personal data transmission would be impossible without cryptography. As with passwords, it is accepted that there is no 'unbreakable' code – just ones that take too long to be worth the effort.

Draw around the hands of a few friends to see how finger length and spacing biometric dimensions can differ between individuals.

1. What would be the best form of biometric security for a computer system? Why?
2. Why are software updates sometimes valued by software companies but not popular with users?

Wider impact of digital technology

In the exam you will be expected to have thought about more than just the separate subject areas: you will need to have a supported (by evidence) opinion on issues such as the ones on these pages. There are questions here to help you think about your answers.

Ethics

Is anonymity a 'good' thing? What about the 'trolls' on social media?

The EU 'right to be forgotten' rules are said to be helping people put right what was incorrect – but is it also helping criminals? Whose rights should be prioritised?

If you store your files online (on someone else's computer) how is your security of data maintained? Is cloud computing the answer to our local problems, or does it provide problems of its own?

Access to online resources

Is it fair that only those who can pay for access in the first place are able to gain the special online offers, while people too poor to pay for access must pay more?

Uneven broadband access based on geography – simply where you live can define your mobile phone and broadband speed and connectivity. Is this fair?

Privacy

Identity theft is a growing business. How should this be dealt with?

With GPS in so many items – is it impossible to be 'away from everyone'? Is this a bad thing?

Wearable tech

A piece of tech that monitors your heartrate might be valuable if you are at risk of heart attack – but what if it is hacked?

If someone wears or has implanted a computer system that helps them perform better – is that cheating?

Computer-based decisions

The driverless car: in an accident, when there is a choice between hitting a wall and possibly killing the car occupants, or hitting a pedestrian in the road – which should the algorithm choose? Why? On what criteria should this choice be made?

Are we slowly expecting more of computers, and less of ourselves?

Legal copyright

If so much can be simply stolen, or at best 'taken for free', does it matter that **copyright** isn't respected? Should electronic files be available to be downloaded regardless of cost or development? How do we pay for the people to do the work if we don't buy the access to the product?

Hacking

Does it matter if systems can be hacked? How do we protect ourselves? What should organisations do when our data held by them is compromised?

The law

You MUST know the main provisions of:

➤ **Data Protection Act (1998)**

Only applies to data about *living* people, known as **personal data**.

Eight data protection principles:

Data should be fairly and lawfully processed

Data should only be used or disclosed for the specified notified purposes

Data should be adequate, relevant and not excessive

Data should be accurate and kept up to date

Data should not be kept any longer than necessary

Access must be provided for individuals to check and correct their data, with a right of explanation when a computer takes automated decisions based on the data

Data should not be transferred outside the European Union except to countries with adequate data protection legislation

➤ **Freedom of Information Act (2000); (Scotland 2002)**

This Act allows the public a right to information held by public authorities such as central and local government, the NHS, education and the police. All requests must be handled within 20 working days, giving reasons if they refuse the request. There are over 20 codified reasons for rejection of requests.

➤ **Computer Misuse Act (1990)**

This is aimed specifically at the offence of hacking and computer misuse. The Act relates to hardware and software, making it a crime not only to access a system without authorisation, but also to edit or access data on that system.

➤ **Copyright, Designs & Patents Act (1988)**

This gives the creators of musical, literary, dramatic and artistic work the right to control how their product is used for a set period. Names often aren't considered copyright, but otherwise if the product is believed to be original, and showing the result of skill and effort, the work can be copyrighted. Products like vacuum cleaners are often patented so that any element of the design used by another company without permission can result in a law suit.

KEYWORDS

Copyright ➤ Refers to the right of the creator of a product to control how it is used

Personal data ➤ Data held by organisations about living people

1. Why is it important to consider the ethics of things we do using computers and the Internet?
2. Would using a computer controlled company toaster for an illicit bagel against company rules break the Computer Misuse Act?
3. Does a 14-year-old have the right to request a copy of their data under the Data Protection Act?

Introduction to encryption

This has already been mentioned in a number of chapters so here is where all of the information is pulled together.

Encryption is the process of converting **plaintext** (original, unencrypted) into **ciphertext** (encrypted) so that the message is as close to impossible to work out as makes no difference. It is accepted that no cipher is unbreakable – but if the cipher key is only used for a set number of hours, and it will take longer than that to break it, then it is secure enough.

Encryption isn't encoding – if you encode something you are changing it into another format, such as Male = M, Female = F: hardly a top secret action. ASCII encodes the letters you type into numbers that the computer can process. So encoding helps the transfer of data.

Encryption is designed to focus the transfer of data to only those who have the key. Anyone else just sees a garbled transmission, such as '95' and doesn't know what this means.

Hashing is used to check whether anyone has tried to break the code before sending it on. Any changes to anything in the content will produce a garbled or changed message when the legitimate key is used.

A simple cipher

One of the simplest encryption systems is known as the Caesar cipher – used by Julius Caesar to communicate with his armies. This is a simple 'shift' cipher, whereby each letter represents another in a logical sequence.

It's easier to see it like this:

A	B	C	D	E	F	G	H	I	J	K	L	M	N	O	P	Q	R	S	T	U	V	W	X	Y	Z
W	X	Y	Z	A	B	C	D	E	F	G	H	I	J	K	L	M	N	O	P	Q	R	S	T	U	V

The top row are the letters we will use for our plaintext message: the bottom row still contains the same letters, but they have been 'shifted' five places to the right. Using this simple cipher, the word 'computing' becomes:

C	O	M	P	U	T	I	N	G
Y	K	I	L	Q	P	E	J	C

Clearly this is fairly easy to break, and you can make it more complex by changing the letters in the encryption to numbers:

C	O	M	P	U	T	I	N	G
25	11	9	12	17	16	5	10	3

And then totalling them up – which is the meaning of the 95 at the beginning of this section.

For the exam, knowing how to use a simple cipher is enough – you don't need to be able to translate the more complex work.

In addition to the moral and ethical need to maintain security of data, you will remember that the Data Protection Act requires all organisations to take reasonable measures to prevent loss of data.

Uses of encryption

Organisations will usually have data protection policies which will include encryption: schools will usually encrypt data held on portable devices that staff use, emails that identify students personally, for example.

The most familiar method of encryption for most users will be **SSL – Secure Sockets Layer**, a protocol that uses a key to encrypt data across the Internet using two keys:
1. A public key accessible to all
2. A private key known only to the recipient of the message.

This combination is the only way in which secure communication is possible: pick a global brand like Amazon – how could they have secret keys with every one of their customers?

How SSL works

Your browser connects to the website and requests an identity check from the server, to make sure that the server sends a recognised SSL certificate. If this is part of a list the browser holds, then all is well. If not, the browser will ask the user 'Are you sure you want to deal with these folks? I don't know them!' At this point it is a good idea to pause and check you have typed the correct URL, because this is a hint that something isn't necessarily right. If the certificate is recognised, the URL changes from HTTP to HTTPS and you can continue your session in an encrypted mode.

KEYWORDS

Plaintext ➤ Unencrypted message
Ciphertext ➤ Encoded or encrypted message that an unauthorised person cannot read
Hashing ➤ Validates the content by detecting any modification since encryption

 Make a simple Caesar cipher using two rulers, each with the alphabet on them, shifting one to change the code.

1. Use a simple five shift right Caesar cipher to encrypt the word EXAMINATION. What is the result?
2. What is the difference between encoding and encryption?

Mind map

Cyber security and ethics

- Cyber threats
  - Definition
    - Protect systems and data from unauthorised access
    - Protect systems and data from attack
  - Types of threat
    - Removable media
      - USB devices
      - Bluetooth
    - Malicious code
      - Viruses
      - Worms
      - Trojan horses
      - Malware
    - Poor access rights config.
      - Use admin login when not needed
      - User profile not deleted when they leave
      - Setting only the rights needed – nothing more
    - Poor password practice
      - Not changed frequently
      - Predictable
      - Repeated across systems
      - Left at default
    - Unpatched/outdated software
      - Old versions
      - Deferred patches
    - Social engineering
      - Blagging
      - Phishing
      - Pharming
      - Shouldering

- Internet of things
  - Wearable tech
  - Smart home
  - Driverless car

- Legal
  - Data Protection Act
  - Computer Misuse Act
  - Freedom of Information Act
  - Copyright, Design & Patents Act

- Your point of view
  - What do you think?
  - What evidence supports your view?
  - What evidence contradicts your view?

- Ethics
  - Anonymity
  - Access
  - Privacy
  - Rights and responsibilities

- Cyber defence
  - Defence strategies
    - Biometrics
      - Fingerprints most common
      - Eye/retina scans
      - Hand or palm geometry
      - Typing or voice recognition
    - Password systems
    - CAPTCHA/reboot CAPTCHA
    - Email confirmation
    - Automatic update software
  - Penetration testing
    - Can be a strategy for defence as well as attack
      - White box
      - Black box

If you need more space to answer the following questions, please use a separate piece of paper.

1. Identify the difference between malware and adware. **(1 mark)**

_____

2. A teacher is using photocopies of a book for a presentation in assembly, and has forgotten to identify the source of the copies. What law is being broken? **(1 mark)**

_____

3. What is the difference between 'blagging' and 'phishing'? **(2 marks)**

_____

_____

4. If a school chooses to back up its data to the United States of America, is it breaking the Data Protection Act? Explain your answer. **(2 marks)**

_____

_____

5. Identify a limitation of CAPTCHA. **(1 mark)**

_____

6. What security option would you recommend for a teacher's laptop to protect the data on it from theft? Explain your answer, comparing at least two systems. **(5 marks)**

_____

_____

_____

_____

_____

7. How do updates help you protect your computer against security threats? **(3 marks)**

_____

_____

_____

8. Consider three technical reasons why social networking sites may have been used by large groups of people around the world to organise protests. **(6 marks)**

_____

_____

_____

_____

_____

ASCII table

Character	Decimal number	Binary number	Character	Decimal number	Binary number
blank space	32	0010 0000	^	94	0101 1110
!	33	0010 0001	-	95	0101 1111
"	34	0010 0010	'	96	0110 0000
#	35	0010 0011	a	97	0110 0001
$	36	0010 0100	b	98	0110 0010
A	65	0100 0001	c	99	0110 0011
B	66	0100 0010	d	100	0110 0100
C	67	0100 0011	e	101	0110 0101
D	68	0100 0100	f	102	0110 0110
E	69	0100 0101	g	103	0110 0111
F	70	0100 0110	h	104	0110 1000
G	71	0100 0111	i	105	0110 1001
H	72	0100 1000	j	106	0110 1010
I	73	0100 1001	k	107	0110 1011
J	74	0100 1010	l	108	0110 1100
K	75	0100 1011	m	109	0110 1101
L	76	0100 1100	n	110	0110 1110
M	77	0100 1101	o	111	0110 1111
N	78	0100 1110	p	112	0111 0000
O	79	0100 1111	q	113	0111 0001
P	80	0101 0000	r	114	0111 0010
Q	81	0101 0001	s	115	0111 0011
R	82	0101 0010	t	116	0111 0100
S	83	0101 0011	u	117	0111 0101
T	84	0101 0100	v	118	0111 0110
U	85	0101 0101	w	119	0111 0111
V	86	0101 0110	x	120	0111 1000
W	87	0101 0111	y	121	0111 1001
X	88	0101 1000	z	122	0111 1010

Fundamentals of Algorithms
Quick test questions
Pages 4–5
1. An algorithm is a set of steps, or instructions, to complete a task, such as a recipe or a washing machine program.
2. An efficient algorithm only uses the resources it absolutely needs to complete the task – no more, no less.
3. The main components of algorithms are INPUTS – PROCESS – OUTPUTS.
4. When you use a trace table you go through your code as if you are the computer, writing down the inputs, the processing and the outputs. This is an essential part of testing, and can help you see where the computer code would go wrong before you even enter it, which saves time in class – and money in business.

Pages 6–7
1. Binary search, because the book will be huge and it will be in a sorted order (alphabetical). Splitting the range searched is more effective.
2. Start with all numbers 22, 19, 17, 15, 2, 9. Sort so that the last two numbers are in order and check the middle number. The middle one is 17.
3. Binary

Pages 8–9
1. Both will produce the answer, but bubble sort may take a lot longer.
2. Compare 22 and 19, OK, compare 19 and 17, OK, compare 15 and 2, OK, compare 2 and 9, swap 9 before 2 and start again. When comparing 9 and 2, OK, sort complete. 22, 19, 17, 15, 9, 2. The list is fully checked again before the computer declares it is sorted.
3. Merge

Exam practice questions
Page 11
1.

Line	Number	i	Output
1	5		
2			5
3		1	
4	8		
5		4	
6			8
3		2	
4	11		
5			11
3		3	
4	14		
5			14

(8 marks: 1 mark per correct answer)

2. **Answers such as:**
   - Establish size of vehicle.
   - Set spray for soap.
   - Set brush height based on sensor settings.
   - Set water jet bar height based on sensor settings.
   - Set fan bar height based on sensor settings.

   (5 marks: 1 mark for each point made)

3. **Answers such as:**
   - Clear out all hiding places (e.g. under bed) and place items in their correct storage locations.
   - Clear out all horizontal spaces (including bottom of wardrobe) and place items in their correct storage locations.
   - Return all items not belonging in the room to their rightful locations.
   - Dust and vacuum. **(2 marks for four points made)**

4. Decomposition helps programmers because once a task has been decomposed it can be tackled one element at a time **(1)**, and the code can be produced one module at a time **(1)**, so they can test each section more effectively **(1)**.

5. 1. Removing non-essential detail allows focus on the core problem. **(1)**
   2. A plan could go down the wrong path, solving the wrong problem. **(1)**
   3. Identifying common elements that can be combined to help design a simpler solution. **(1)**

6. It prints the numbers 1–10. **(2)**

7. • Effectively using the computer resources available at the time.
   • Using the minimum amount of steps or code.
   • The least possible time for the program to run.
   (3 marks: 1 mark for each point made)

8. The binary search approach chooses the middle value in a sorted array **(1)**, and works out whether the value sought is higher or lower – moving up or down the list **(1)** to locate what it seeks. This means that the computer only ever searches half of the data, because it is either on the right number, or pointed at the right half of the data that is in the array. A linear search is used when you can't sort the data into any useful order **(1)**, or when there are very few items to search. This is because it is also known as 'brute force' searching **(1)**. The computer searches from the first item until either the end of the data **(1)**, or until the item sought is located, one by one. This can take a really, really long time, which is why it is used only when a binary search isn't possible or appropriate.

9. Merge sort is also known as 'divide and conquer' **(1)** because like the binary search the merge sort splits the data in half, sorts the smaller groups, and then merges the two together again. Bubble sort comes from the way that stones settle in a tank of bubbling water **(1)**: the smaller ones 'sink' to the bottom of the tank while the large ones appear to rise to the top. That is why sometimes a bubble sort is called a sinking sort **(1)**. Bubble sort is horrendously long-winded, which is why it is only useful for very small volumes of data.

Programming 1
Quick test questions
Pages 12–13
1. A digital data = on/off, true/false
2. Any WHOLE number.
3. Iteration is repetition of a process or sequence of instructions. This will help a programmer because, for example, they can write the code to check for the temperature value once and set the computer up to test for a set value continually.

Pages 14–15
1. Organise everything together
   Plug in a kettle
   Put teabag in cup
   Put water into kettle
   Switch on kettle
   Wait for kettle to boil
   Add water to cup
   Remove teabag with spoon
   Add milk and/or sugar
   Serve
2. Pseudocode is closest to natural English of all the languages used in Computer Science. We use it to structure our planning before writing the code for real. It is not written in full sentences, like natural English, but in code structure. Computers do not understand pseudocode.
3. FOR is count controlled, WHILE is context controlled. FOR is set to the limits designed by the programmer, FOR temp>20; but WHILE depends on the conditions.

Pages 16–17

1. 11/2 Mod operation = 1
   11/2 Div operation = 5
2. 5+2 = 7, 12/3 = 4
   7 * 4 = 28
3. IF temp = hot
         Cold drink
   ELSE
         Hot drink

Pages 18–19

1.

2.

3.

Exam practice questions

Page 21

1. (a) Counter is an integer. **(1)**
   (b) (i) Variable is a storage location in memory which
       can hold data and is given a unique name by
       the programmer. In the code above, counter is a
       variable. **(1)**
       (ii) Iteration is the repeated operation of a sequence
        of statements in a code. In this example the code
        iterates 11 times and on the final time, when the
        counter value equals 11, it falls to the 'all done'
        output. **(1)**
       (iii) An algorithm is a sequence of instructions to
        complete a task in a set number of steps. In the code
        above the algorithm counts from 1 to 10, then prints
        'all done'. **(1)**
2. Named subroutines, constants and variables are easier for
   human programmers to track **(1)** and check effectively: the
   computer doesn't know the difference. Being quickly able to
   see where a particular subroutine is located can enable faster
   upgrades and debugging **(1)**.
3. A variable is 'assigned' when it is given a name and a value
   by the programmer. **(1)**
4. Definite iteration has a specific limit **(1)**, such as 'For I = 1 – 10'.
   Indefinite iteration is seen with WHILE commands because the
   computer will run that section of code until something else
   happens **(1)**, so 'WHILE temp >20, print "Warm"' will print
   the same thing for as long as the temperature is greater than
   20 degrees, regardless of how long that is.
5. IF GameOver THEN
         SCORE = PlayerSCORE
         IF SCORE > TOPSCORE THEN
               TOPSCORE = SCORE
               PRINT "Genius"
         ENDIF
         PRINT "Game Over: See you next time!"
   ENDIF

   **(1 mark for variables; 1 mark for completed code that
   shows the nested IF; 1 mark for clear ends to IF loops)**
6. Within a program, using the AND function means two
   conditions must be met to achieve a certain output but the
   NOT function means the opposite of any condition is returned. **(1)**

Programming 2
Quick test questions
Pages 22–23

1. Any individual detail such as first name, surname, address,
   phone number, date of birth.
2. Just the names [Fred; Alfie; Oscar]
3. Using a key, value combination in a two-dimensional array:
   Pets(0,0) = "Fred", Pets(0,1) = "Dachshund", Pets(1,0) =
   "Alfie", Pets(1,1) = "Labradoodle",
   Pets(2,0) = "Oscar", Pets(2,1) = "Terrier"

Pages 24–25

1. Write means you want to write new data or overwrite existing
   data, read means just look at it.
2. Because it takes more memory, more time to load, and allows
   more possibility of error through accidental edit or delete.

Pages 26–27

1. For example:

Convert string to integer	Int(string)
Convert integer to string	Str(4)
Convert string to real	Float(4.01)
Convert real to string	Str(0.5)
Convert content of string to upper case	string.toUpper(fred)
Convert content of string to lower case	string.toLower(fred)

2. If you were translating words from one language to another using a keyboard which does not have the same character set: you can just type the number; if you were checking that a page is laid out correctly and wanted to check how many spaces had been used in a line.

3. 'Sc'

Pages 28–29

1. Cryptography, simulations, gaming, gambling, science

2. Without limits, an unnecessarily large or small number could be generated

Pages 30–31

1. One-to-many – while she has only one Form Group, that Form Group will have more than one student.

2. A record holds all the information or data about one specific object that has been entered into the database. Each individual element of information in the record – such as a telephone number or hair colour – is referred to as a field.

Exam practice questions
Page 33

1. Two-dimensional arrays allow more complex data to be stored than simple lists, or one-dimensional arrays.
   A one-dimensional array:

Index	0	1	2	3	4	5	6	7	8
Value	2	4	6	8	10	12	14	16	18

A 2-dimensional array is 'an array of arrays', and is best shown on a 2 dimensional table:

	0	1	2
0	2	8	14
1	4	10	16
2	6	12	18

(4 marks: 1 mark for each definition; 1 mark for each example)

2. **(a)** Any of the rows – Smith, Jones, Hassan or Cengiz. **(1)**
   (b) Primary key would be the employee number, because it is unique to each employee and not duplicated anywhere. **(2)**
   (c) Any reasonable number, below 30 and above 15, would be acceptable: enough space is needed for longer surnames **(1)** but not so long that space is wasted in the database **(1)**.

3. • Relational DB
   • Search and sort options
   • Link to customer database
   • Expandable
   (4 marks: 1 mark for each point made)

4. ASCII CODE **(3)**

5. Unicode accounts for the variety of character sets **(1)** used by non-Western languages by adding to the original content **(1)**.

Programming 3
Quick test questions
Pages 34–35

1. Washing machine; dishwasher; DVD player; thermostat-controlled heating; burglar alarm

2. Depends on answer to 1. For example, DVD player: eject carrier/seek disk presence/seek initial contents of disk/load context/play/dismount disk on stop command.

Pages 36–37

1. Global: it is referenced throughout the code.

2. They can be affected by the code in ways that aren't always predictable and you can end up with a variable that isn't the value you expect. Global variables are also held in memory causing an additional, if usually small, burden on the computer.

Pages 38–39

1. **(a)** OUTPUT "ENTER DATE OF BIRTH"
   IF DATEOFBIRTH–CURRENTDATE = >13
   OUTPUT "WELCOME"
   (b) It would include those who WERE 13 as well as those older than 13.
   (c) You have no idea if the user is telling the truth.

Exam practice questions
Page 41

1. The code can be written once, then used more than once **(1)**, as needed **(1)**. You can access and use any variable **(1)** from your main code without having to redefine **(1)** it.

2. Structured programming is an approach that forces a logical structure on the code **(1)**. Clearly breaking a big task into little **(1)** ones makes the big task more achievable, using code modules or subroutines (one for each part of the task) makes it easy to see which part of the code does which part of the overall task **(1)**, updates are a lot easier – you just change the bit that needs to be updated.

3. **Any three from the following:** source code is more easily understood when the elements are defined where they are needed; global variables can change value at different points so it is harder to keep track of them; sometimes global variables can become tangled because they are called at conflicting points in the program; it is much easier to test the code and the variable if you can do this in modules; can reduce memory required at any given time. **(3 marks: 1 mark for each point made)**

4. When a program passes data to a procedure or function, the parameters in the procedure or function handle that data **(1)** so the procedure or function can perform operations on the data **(1)**. Usually parameters are included in parentheses () **(1)** after the command, such as:
   int Total;
   int cost = 40;
   int VAT= 2;
   Total = sum(cost, VAT)

5. Data validation checks that data is reasonable **(1)**, within defined limits **(1)**, such as SchoolAge>5<20, but doesn't check if a user is telling the truth **(1)** or whether the data input is accurate **(1)**. Verification checks that the input is accurate, comparing against a record in a database.

6. Test data should cover normal (typical) **(1)**, boundary (extreme) **(1)** and erroneous data **(1)**. Normal data is what the program would use regularly **(1)** and therefore it should accept this with no errors; boundary data is on the edge of the range that is acceptable **(1)**. Erroneous data, such as FRED entered in an age field, should always be thrown back **(1)**.

7. High-level languages are closest to human language: they need a compiler because the computer doesn't understand them, which also means they are slower to run. They are easy to modify because we can read them quickly. Most code is written in these because they can be designed for a specific purpose and are easier to use.
   Low-level languages are closest to the way the computer operates: these are also the oldest and hardest to use. Only specific tasks are written in these because they are complex to operate, but they run faster because they're already in a language the computer can use. They are harder to write and harder to update, so only specialists tend to use them. **(6 marks: 1 point for each point made)**

Fundamentals of Data Representation
Quick test questions
Pages 42–43

1. **Any one from:** hexadecimal is easier (for humans) to read (than binary); hexadecimal is easier to convert (to binary) than decimal; numbers are displayed in a more compact way (in hexadecimal than in binary); it is quicker to type in (hexadecimal numbers than binary numbers); it is more accurate to type in (hexadecimal numbers than binary numbers).

2. bit, nibble, byte

3. In decimal this is 26 + 9,
   00^10^111010
   $+ \underline{0\,0\,01001}$
   $0\,1\,00011$
   35

Pages 44–45

1. For example, a 64 MB hard drive would be 64*1024*1024 bytes – 67108864 bytes.
2. It extends the ASCII character set to include non-Western characters.
3. 81

Pages 46–47

1. Advantages. Good quality image and shows details and range of colours.
   Disadvantages. Takes much longer to download, could stop the rest of the page downloading while it blocks traffic and can annoy users.
2. They are useful where the detail isn't the important thing, such as a map or geometric shape, where compression won't damage the product.

Pages 48–49

1. (a) This will depend on your name, but generally Huffman coding will produce a much smaller file size than simple ASCII because each letter in ASCII is 7 bits before you start. For example, the name Anna would be as follows: ANNA 2A 2N so A could be 0 and N could be 1, using two bits to code the letters
   (b) For example ANNA would be 65 78 78 65 – taking up 4 bytes of space.

Exam practice questions
Page 51

1. 190 **(1)**
2. 1 **(1)**
3. 18 **(1)**
4. 10100 – 1000, = 01100, or C **(1)**
5. 63 **(1)**
6. 01100000 **(1)**
7. 5 **(1)**
8. The computer only sees the ASCII code **(1)** not the letter so there has to be a different code for each letter **(1)**. The computer outputs the code associated with the letter **(1)**, and in human readable output we use uppercase and lowercase letters.
9.

0	1	1	1	0
0	1	0	0	0
0	1	1	1	0
0	1	0	0	0
0	1	1	1	0

01110 01000 01110 01000 01110 **(3 marks: 1 mark for each 'half' of the shape; 1 mark for the sequence)**
10. 16 possible colours **(1)**
11. The program takes a number of samples of the sound at set intervals **(1)**, and works out the 'top' and 'bottom' **(1)** values of the analogue sound. If the sound being processed is 'above' the halfway point, the program checks again **(1)** if the sound would still be above halfway if the first half was cut into half again, and so on. 'Above' is recorded as a '1', 'below' it is recorded as a '0'. The number of times this is checked is reflected in what is called the bitrate **(1)**. These questions change the number of 'steps' that replace the smooth sine wave: again, as with graphics, the more bits the better the quality – and the larger the file **(1)**.

Computer Systems
Quick test questions
Pages 52–53

1. OR
2. AND

Pages 54–55

1. AV just protects you from wandering virus programs, a firewall protects you from attack from an external source, such as a hacker.

2. This depends on the two you select: GUI systems are generally more user-friendly but tend to be locked down so CLI systems are often preferred by people who want to 'tweak' settings. GUI systems are more popular and more expensive – most CLI are open-source and can therefore be tailored for bespoke systems, while a generic GUI tries to be a jack of all trades.
3. Utility programs are designed with a single purpose in mind, such as clearing out unused files. They work with your OS.
4. The operating system manages all of the computer resources.

Pages 56–57

1. This depends on the task, on the cores and on the RAM amount and speed.
2. This is when an 'instruction fetch' and 'data operation' cannot occur at the same time because they use the same bus which can only transfer data one way at a time.
3. Every piece of data has to transfer across the same bus, so the data transfer speed is slow and the CPU spends a lot of time sitting waiting for the next thing. The data transfer speed needs to be flexible rather than set, since some data is needed faster than others. Data and programs share the same space, so corrupted programs could make a mess of the data stored.

Pages 58–59

1. This is a matter of personal preference:
   There is greater capacity in cloud storage, though large files take longer to upload for backup in the first place. There is a question over ownership and security of files stored in the cloud. Local data is cheap to purchase now but exactly because it is stored locally you cannot access your data on the move.
2. Because it is cheap, because we don't need it to hold contents for a long time: volatile memory is used as a scribbleboard that we wipe ready for the next task. It is fast access memory that can respond to the needs of the CPU processing.

Exam practice questions
Page 61

1. Any three from: microphone; computer cable connection; SD card; wireless; Bluetooth. **(3 marks: 1 mark for each point made)**
2. **Any two from the following:**
   (i) Difference: No moving parts in solid state media
       Explanation: Magnetic media are often unsuitable for mobile use because the mechanical parts cannot function during movement/mechanical parts are less robust during movement.
   (ii) Difference: Faster read access in solid state drives than magnetic.
       Explanation: Data can often be read more quickly from solid state media than magnetic media.
   (iii) Difference: Solid state media can be more compact than magnetic media.
       Explanation: The smaller size enables better portability.
   (iv) Difference: Less heat generated when using solid state.
       Explanation: Uses less power OR allows the product to be smaller. **(3 marks: 1 mark for each difference; 1 mark for the explanation)**
3. False **(1)**
4. Q is OFF **(2 marks: 1 mark for Q identified; 1 mark for OFF)**
5. The computer has memory that can hold data and the program **(1)** (nowadays called RAM).
   The control unit manages the process of moving the data **(1)** and program between memory and storage – in the VN design this is called the 'accumulator' **(1)**.
   The ALU is the calculator in the model **(1)**. It also operates relative calculations such as 'less than'.
   The bus indicates the flow of data **(1)** between each component and is shown as arrows on the diagram.

6. The CPU reads (fetches) instructions **(1)** from the memory cache, or RAM **(1)**, decodes them, and then operates – or executes **(1)** – the instruction.
7. A large amount of RAM enables more instructions/programs to be loaded from secondary storage into RAM **(1)** so they can be executed by the processor more efficiently rather than the CPU needing to wait for the instruction to be located and loaded. As a result more programs may be run simultaneously. Additionally, some programs simply need a lot of RAM to run properly **(1)**, such as games programs.
8. The cloud is a colloquial term for 'the Internet' and is often also defined as 'other people's computers'. The advantages for many businesses include that:
   Storage is flexible and cheaper than purchasing and managing the hardware onsite.
   Offices across the world can access the same files.
   Local disaster recovery is easier – as long as your storage provider wasn't the one hit. **(3 marks: 1 mark for each point made)**

Fundamentals of Computer Networks
Quick test questions
Pages 62–63
1. This depends on the size of the network and the composition, but most schools are star network because this is the most stable and can be most easily extended.
2. Generally anyone mobile is better off with wireless tech if they are moving about (the DJ and their microphone for example) but if they are working static (like a photographer) then they can use wired and benefit from the faster and more secure data transfer.

Pages 64–65
1. If they're on a tight budget, a bus network would probably give them the flexibility of access to resources that they need. That said, it is vulnerable to all sorts of crashes, so a ring would be a better choice, with a star the best and most flexible option.
2. A whitelist is stronger because it blocks everything first, and then checks whether that connection is allowed. A blacklist allows everything first, then checks whether the connection is allowed.

Pages 66–67
1. File Transfer Protocol.
2. True
3. IMAP leaves a copy of the message on the server, SMTP draws the files down to the local machine.

Exam practice questions
Page 69
1. Wired, where the computers are stationary **(1)** to ensure security **(1)**; then wireless for all portable devices to ensure that their main asset – portability- is maintained. This will help limit the opportunities for hacking, especially if the WEP password is changed on the router **(1)**.
2. When there are very few workstations on the network **(1)**, and all resources are easily shared **(1)**.
3. This makes data appear meaningless **(1)** and provides security **(1)** for the content both when stored electronically and when transmitted using an encryption key. This is particularly important when storing and/or transmitting personal data (Data Protection Act).
4. A whitelist identifies authorised sites **(1)** if on an Internet filter, or users or machines if on a firewall **(1)**. Only those on the whitelist are allowed through. This is more secure than the opposite blacklist **(1)** because that simply bars only those entities identified on the list: the whitelist bars everything *except* what is on the list **(1)**.
5. This refers to the balancing of workload between the user's computer (client) and the host computer (server) **(1)** so that the transaction is concluded more quickly **(1)**. Generally the server computer is more powerful, so it holds user data and does the harder work.
6. WAN, group of WANs, group of Stars, mesh of Stars **(1)**.

7.
```
┌─────────────────────────────┐
│      APPLICATION LAYER       │
└─────────────────────────────┘

┌─────────────────────────────┐
│      TRANSPORT LAYER         │
└─────────────────────────────┘

┌─────────────────────────────┐
│      INTERNET LAYER          │
└─────────────────────────────┘

┌─────────────────────────────┐
│      NETWORK ACCESS          │
│   (or DATA LINK) LAYER       │
└─────────────────────────────┘
```
(4 marks: 1 mark for each completed entry)
8. Ring **(1)**

Cyber Security and Ethics
Quick test questions
Pages 70–71
1. Because USB storage is unreliable since it can be used in a number of different devices, and because the software on the device might be malicious, so the software could copy itself across devices using the USB storage as a transport – unless the system is secured it will be vulnerable to any threat from outside.
2. Yes – corrupting software that allows access to network files can be transferred to a computer system through a removable device: a firewall would question the unauthorised access.
3. It pretends to come from a legitimate source, such as a bank, and asks for your details.

Pages 72–73
1. This depends on the system – fingerprint is cheapest and often the most reliable, but wouldn't suit a top-secret vault: the more secure eye or retinal scan would suit if money is no object.
2. Software companies prefer to be able to update software on time to avoid the poor reputation of being vulnerable to malicious attack. This isn't always at a time that is convenient to the user. There is also sometimes a concern about the amount of personal data available to the company as a result of the arrangement, since all settings have to be visible to their system for the update to take place.

Pages 74–75
1. Because what we do in the electronic or virtual world has effects on the real world, and we can only exist together if we agree what is 'right' and 'wrong'.
2. Yes, if it is computer-controlled with a login system which has been compromised.
3. No – they're not 18, but the adult with responsibility for them can do so.

Pages 76–77
1. J   C   F   R   N   S   F   Y   N   T   S
2. Encoding changes data into a format that can be processed, usually by computers, such as M = Male, F = Female, DOB = Date Of Birth. Encryption changes data into a format which can only be read by those with the key – who should be the authorised recipients of the message.

Exam practice questions
Page 79
1. Malware is designed to damage your code or computer; adware fills your computer with ads, sometimes making them pop up in your browser when you are searching for something online. **(1)**
2. Copyright, Designs & Patents Act. **(1)**

3. Arguably, there is a fine line between these two. Blagging tends to be more personal **(1)** while phishing tends to be pretending to be an organisation **(1)**, but both seek to fool you into giving your personal or confidential details away.

4. No **(1)**. The USA is regarded as having sufficient data security measures in place **(1)**, though this is now a grey area as a result of the revelations about the NSA and GCHQ monitoring Internet transactions.

5. It is hard to read and the 'sound' option often isn't clear enough. **(1)**

6. Biometrics such as retinal scans are the most secure but are also expensive to add to existing hardware and can be difficult to reprogram if and when the teacher leaves the school. A password is the cheapest system, but it can often be the weakest as well if the password is easy to break. Usually the data on a teacher's laptop is encrypted and the teachers are required to change their passwords frequently, so that there is less of a chance that the laptop data will be compromised using this system. **(5 marks: 1 mark for each point made)**

7. Thousands of security threats are discovered in a year **(1)**, and the software companies are always writing code to ensure that their product is resilient **(1)** against the attacks from the threats they discover. If you do not update your computer, then the threat remains **(1)**.

8. **Any three from:** social networking fast to transfer so harder to censor; has a global reach so can reach more people more quickly than other media; lack of central control by a government because the data is stored in another country; allows incorporation of text with images/video/sound. **(6 marks: 1 mark for each comment, 1 mark for explanation of impact)**

Index

GCSE Success

Computer Science

Exam Practice Workbook

Sharon Angland

Contents

Computer systems

Fundamentals of computer networks

Cyber security and ethics

Practice exam papers

ASCII table

Answers

1   Define the term 'algorithm'.   [2 marks]

....

....

2   Explain the purpose of the algorithm set out in this flowchart.   [3 marks]

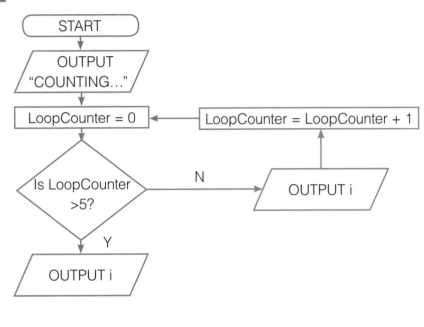

....

....

....

3   Draw a flowchart to describe an algorithm to print all numbers divisible by 3 up to 100.   [5 marks]

For more help on this topic, see Letts GCSE Computer Science Revision Guide pages 4–5.

4 State **two** properties of an algorithm that could be considered when describing it as 'efficient'. [2 marks]

....

....

5 A student needs to open and edit a password-protected file.
Put the following steps into the correct order: [5 marks]

Edit Data ....

Save and Close ....

Enter Password ....

Select Program ....

Select File and Open ....

6 Define 'iteration' in the context of designing a program structure. [1 mark]

....

7 How would a programmer use decomposition when given an initial project brief? [2 marks]

....

....

8 How might we use abstraction to create a clearer 'model' of a problem? [2 marks]

....

....

9 Explain how a trace table is used to test a computer program to check for early errors. [2 marks]

....

....

....

For more help on this topic, see Letts GCSE Computer Science Revision Guide pages 4–5.

1 Explain the steps involved in a binary search. [4 marks]

....

....

....

....

2 Explain how a linear search looks at a data source. [2 marks]

....

....

3 Identify what type of search this is. [1 mark]

```
ClassList= ["Alex", "Riley", "Chris", "Bailey", "Jamie"]
INPUT A #name you're looking for
FOREACH [item in list]:
    IF [item] == A,
        OUTPUT result stop search
    ELSE
        RETURN
END
```

....

4 Linear search is often also known as 'brute force' searching.

Why is this? [1 mark]

....

....

5 Why does a binary search require a sorted dataset? [3 marks]

....

....

....

....

For more help on this topic, see Letts GCSE Computer Science Revision Guide pages 6–7.

6 Explain when a linear search might be more efficient than a binary search. [2 marks]

....

....

7 At first glance, which type of search would be the most appropriate for the following data?

Give a reason for your answer. [2 marks]

> I want to find if there are any '9's in the list:
>
> 1,2,3,4,5,6,7,8,9,10,11,12

....

....

8 Which would be the most appropriate type of search for the following data?

Give a reason for your answer. [2 marks]

> I want to find if there are any Hussains in the class:
>
> "Adams", "Banks", "Kelly", "Madsen", "Lisson", "Hepworth"

....

....

For more help on this topic, see Letts GCSE Computer Science Revision Guide pages 6–7.

1 Which of the following processes describes merge sort? Tick **one** option. [1 mark]

   A Repeatedly splits the data in half until each 'list' contains only a single data item. Then, having broken it into smaller parts, it repeatedly combines these 'lists' back together, this time putting them in their required order (ascending or descending in value). ☐

   B Compares the first two items, checks which one is larger and swaps them if necessary so that the larger is first. Then it checks the next pair, and so on. ☐

2 Use a bubble sort to sort the dataset (6,2,4,1,8) in ascending order. Show your working and state the number of steps required. [4 marks]

....

....

....

....

....

....

....

3 Complete the merge sort example shown. [3 marks]

| 4 | 1 | 9 | 6 |

| 4 | 1 | | | 6 |

| 4 | | | |

1 What is a 'Boolean data type'? [1 mark]

....

2 Explain what type of data a telephone number is. [3 marks]

....

....

3 What is a 'variable'? [3 marks]

....

....

4 What is the value of a at the end of this code segment? [1 mark]

```
a = 0
for i = 1 to 5
    a = a+1
next i
print a
```

....

5 What does the phrase 'constant declaration' mean, and how is it different from declaring a variable? [4 marks]

....

....

....

6 'Repeat' instructions like the one below are an example of which technique? [1 mark]
(NB fd = 'forward'; 'rt' = 'right' followed by the degrees to turn)

```
Repeat 360 [fd 1 rt 1]
```

....

7 Identify the benefit to the programmer of iteration in a code. [4 marks]

....

....

....

For more help on this topic, see Letts GCSE Computer Science Revision Guide pages 12–13.

Module 4

1 Give a definition of 'pseudocode'. [2 marks]

2 Write the pseudocode for a simple algorithm that is used to process data entered by a class teacher. It prints 'passed' if a student's mark is above 30, and 'did not pass' if it isn't. [2 marks]

3 Explain what the following code does. [3 marks]

```
n=0
while n<=100
    display n
    n=n+1
endwhile
```

For more help on this topic, see Letts GCSE Computer Science Revision Guide pages 14–15.

4 Explain what the following code does. [3 marks]

```
input startnumber, finish
if startnumber > finish
      print error message
else
      for n=startnumber to finishnumber
          print n
      next
endif
```

....

....

....

....

5 Write the pseudocode to take three numbers as input and print the sum
and product of those numbers. [3 marks]

....

....

....

....

....

....

For more help on this topic, see Letts GCSE Computer Science Revision Guide pages 14–15.

1 Write a simple program to multiply two user input numbers together, and print the result. [1 mark]

....

....

....

....

2 Explain why the following two codes would display and produce different results. [3 marks]

Code 1	Code 2
a = 13	a = 13
b = 2	b = 2
c = INT(a/b)	c = FLOAT(a/b)
print c	print c

....

....

....

....

....

3 Explain why the calculation in this program would cause a problem. [1 mark]

```
input Name
input Age
Score =
Name*Age
Print Score
```

....

....

For more help on this topic, see Letts GCSE Computer Science Revision Guide pages 16–17.

4 The following code aims to work out overtime pay.

Describe why it is incorrect. [2 marks]

```
Input EmployeeName
Input HoursWorked
Input HourRate
Input OvertimeWorked
Input OvertimeRate
pay = (HoursWorked / HourRate) + (OvertimeWorked * OvertimeRate)
print pay
End
```

5 State what the output and result of this code would be. [2 marks]

```
a = 15
b = 23
IF a < 10 AND b < 50
    print "Class Dismissed"
ELSE
    print "Extra Homework!"
ENDIF
```

6 If line three in question 5 is changed to: [2 marks]

```
IF a >= 10 AND b < 50
    print "Class Dismissed"
```

what will be the result, and why?

For more help on this topic, see Letts GCSE Computer Science Revision Guide pages 16–17.

1 What do the following flowchart symbols mean? [4 marks]

a   b   c   d

a = ...

b = ...

c = ...

d = ...

2 Describe what the following flowchart does. [4 marks]

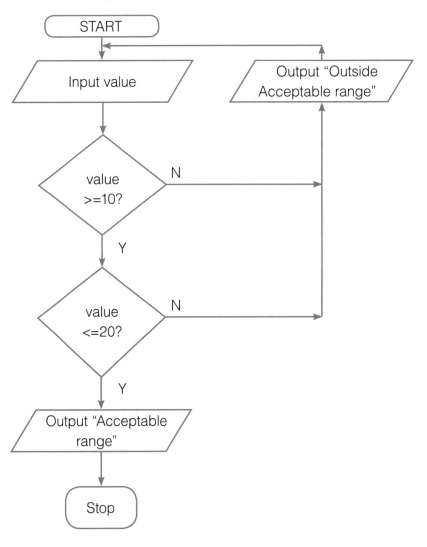

For more help on this topic, see Letts GCSE Computer Science Revision Guide pages 18–19.

3 Put the flowchart elements below in the correct order to monitor the temperature in a greenhouse.

[2 marks]

For more help on this topic, see Letts GCSE Computer Science Revision Guide pages 18–19.

1 Black and white bitmap images can be encoded using 1 to represent white and 0 to represent black in a two-dimensional array. Show the two dimensional array for the capital letter C where the array is 4 pixels by 4 pixels. [2 marks]

2 In programming, what are 'data structures'? [2 marks]

....

....

3 If a list contains the following elements, what would be output by the command `print(text[2])` if the array count starts at [0]? Give a reason for your answer. [2 marks]

> text = ["apples"; "oranges"; "pears"; "bananas"]

4 Is this acceptable data for an array? Give a reason for your answer. [2 marks]

> names = ["Max","Khali",22,"Sam")

5 If a two-dimensional array is defined as below, identify how many elements are contained within it. [2 marks]

> myArray(6,6)

6 In the list below, identify the item at index point [5] if the index starts at [0]. [1 mark]

> (1,2,3,4,5,6,7,8,9)

7 What do programmers mean when they describe an array as 'static'? [1 mark]

For more help on this topic, see Letts GCSE Computer Science Revision Guide pages 22–23.

1 Describe what this code would do. [4 marks]

```
file = open("contacts.csv", "a")
name = input("Please enter name.")
phone = input("Please enter phone number.")
file.write(name + "," + phone + "\n")
```

....

....

2 Describe **two** ways external data can be collected. [2 marks]

....

....

....

3 Describe how an index aids file handling. [2 marks]

....

....

4 Explain why it is possible for someone to enter a chatroom for 20-year-olds and be only 15. [2 marks]

....

....

5 Complete the code below to add a new name to a class list. [2 marks]

```
file = open("classlist.csv", "a")

.............................. = input("Please enter name.")

file. ..............................  (name + ","+ "\n")
```

6 If a file is opened, edited, saved and closed on a daily basis, identify a limitation of this method and a possible solution. [2 marks]

....

....

....

For more help on this topic, see Letts GCSE Computer Science Revision Guide pages 24–25.

1   Define the data type 'string'.   [2 marks]

2   Complete the following table to show which data you would store as an integer and which you would store as a string.

Tick **one** box in each row.   [4 marks]

Data type	Store as an integer	Store as a string
Steve		
15		
007		
2010		
10.2		
01501 2987659		

3   If the following variables are given string values, what would be the result when they were concatenated in the same order in which they were entered?

Give a reason for your answer.   [2 marks]

```
one = "fish"
two = "chips"
three = "mushy peas"
```

4   A string can also be an array of characters:

```
one = ["f", "i", "s", "h"]
```

If a function returns the numeric character code, and the character code for one[1] is 105 and the character code for one[3] is 104, what is the character code for one[0]?   [1 mark]

5   Explain why a character encoding system uses a different code for upper- and lowercase letters.   [1 mark]

For more help on this topic, see Letts GCSE Computer Science Revision Guide pages 26–27.

1 Explain the difference between a random number and a pseudorandom number. [2 marks]

2 Describe **two** modern uses of computer-generated random numbers. [2 marks]

3 Explain what the following code does. How does it use the random feature within the language? [4 marks]

```
import random
My _ number = random.randint(1, 100)
guess = int(input("Take a guess: "))
tries = 1

# guessing loop
while guess != Mynumber:
    if guess > Mynumber:
        print("Too high!")
    else:
        print("Too low!")
    endif
    guess = int(input("What is your guess: "))
    tries += 1
endwhile
print("You got it!  The number was", Mynumber)
print("And it only took you", guesses, "tries!\n")
```

For more help on this topic, see Letts GCSE Computer Science Revision Guide pages 28–29.

1 Explain the difference between a flat file and a relational database. Support your answer with examples. [4 marks]

....

....

....

2 What is the role of a primary key? [1 mark]

....

3 Giving examples, what is the difference between 'structured' and 'unstructured' data? [4 marks]

....

....

....

4 State the purpose of a database report. [1 mark]

....

5 Use the table below to answer the following questions.

StockList				
Product ID	**Product type**	**Colour**	**Size**	**Cost**
A	569875	T-shirt	Blue	S	£14.99
B	258649	Trainers	Black	6	£29.99
C	333548	Hoodie	Red	M	£29.99
D	335948	Shirt	White	M	£12.99
E	798994	Socks	White	5	£6.99
F	222687	Shirt	Blue	M	£12.99

What would be the outcome of these SQL searches?

(a)
```
SELECT * FROM StockList
WHERE Size='M'
AND Colour='White'
```
[1 mark]

(b)
```
SELECT * FROM StockList
WHERE Size='M'
AND ProductType='Shirt'
```
[2 marks]

(c)
```
SELECT * FROM StockList
WHERE Cost<£20.00
```
[4 marks]

For more help on this topic, see Letts GCSE Computer Science Revision Guide pages 30–31.

1 Give **three** reasons why using a structured approach to their code will benefit a programmer. [3 marks]

....

....

....

2 Within structured programming, good programmers plan what they intend to do, then comment the code as it is constructed. In this context, what is a comment? Give an example. [2 marks]

....

....

....

3 Describe the **three** types of translation programming software and provide a brief description of each. [6 marks]

....

....

....

....

....

....

4 Describe the steps a programmer can take to make the code they write easier for another programmer to follow. [4 marks]

1. ....

2. ....

3. ....

4. ....

For more help on this topic, see Letts GCSE Computer Science Revision Guide pages 34–35.

Module 13

1 Name a parameter within this function. [1 mark]

```
FUNCTION Test1(name, value)
    IF name[1] = value
        RETURN true
    ELSE
        RETURN false
    ENDIF
ENDFUNCTION
```

2 Describe **two** examples of using subroutines in a program. [2 marks]

3 A school is developing a part of its website to allow parents and students to upload images. They need a subroutine that would check that the image is within the maximum size allowed (1 MB) before uploading only those that are the right size.

Write a pseudocode subroutine that would do this. [6 marks]

4 Four separate subroutines have been written to control a robot in a factory:

```
FD (x) moves the robot x squares forwards
LT (x) turns the robot x degrees left
RT (x) turns the robot x degrees right
Obstacle() is a Boolean response to the status of the robot
```

For more help on this topic, see Letts GCSE Computer Science Revision Guide pages 36–37.

(a) What would be the path of the robot through the grid below if the following code was executed?

[1 mark]

FD (3)
LT (90)
FD (3)
RT (90)
FD (1)

↑
START

(b) What would be the path of the robot through the grid below if the following code was executed?

[1 mark]

	OBSTACLE			

WHILE Obstacle= TRUE:
FD (1)
LT (90)
FD (4)
RT (90)
ENDWHILE
FD (2)

↑
START

(c) Write the code for the path of the robot through the grid below from **START** to **END**.

[1 mark]

			END

↑
START

....

....

....

For more help on this topic, see Letts GCSE Computer Science Revision Guide pages 36–37.

1 A program is only as good as its data. Explain how validation and verification can help ensure that the data is as 'good' as possible. [6 marks]

....

....

....

....

....

....

2 Describe **one** method of validation used by online surveys to help them manage the quality of their data. [2 marks]

....

....

3 Validation is required for the data in the parameters for the function below:

Function WorkingTime (TimeIn,TimeOut)

Set a test, and show an example of invalid data. [2 marks]

....

....

4 Give **two** reasons why programmers test their code. [2 marks]

1. ....

2. ....

5 A program requires a date of birth from the 20th century to be entered. Provide normal, extreme and erroneous test data examples in the format DD/MM/YYYY. [3 marks]

....

....

....

For more help on this topic, see Letts GCSE Computer Science Revision Guide pages 38–39.

1 Explain why programmers use hexadecimal instead of binary. [3 marks]

....

....

2 What is the decimal representation of the hexadecimal number A2?

Show your working. [2 marks]

....

....

....

3 What is the binary result of 00000111 + 00000111?

Show your working. [2 marks]

....

....

....

4 What is the hexadecimal representation of 256?

Show your working. [2 marks]

....

....

....

....

For more help on this topic, see Letts GCSE Computer Science Revision Guide pages 42–43.

1 Each unit in binary is called a 'bit', and a single bit in binary can represent one of two numbers, 0 and 1.

How many numbers can be represented by:

(a) 3 bits? .... [1 mark]

(b) 8 bits? .... [1 mark]

(c) 12 bits? .... [1 mark]

2 Describe how 1 bit per pixel can be used to represent this image. [1 mark]

....

....

3 If 8 bits are a byte, what are 4 bits? [1 mark]

....

4 If a kilobyte is 1024 bytes and a megabyte (MB) is 1024 kilobytes, fill in the gaps for the following sizes. [2 marks]

A gigabyte (GB) is 1024 ....

A terabyte (TB) is 1024 ....

5 If a robot has a 4-bit instruction set, how many individual different instructions can it operate?

Give a reason for your answer. [2 marks]

....

....

For more help on this topic, see Letts GCSE Computer Science Revision Guide pages 44–45.

6 On a computer monitor, state how many colours are displayed by 8-bit colour. [1 mark]

....

7 Define 'colour depth' and state how it affects file size. [2 marks]

....

....

....

8 Give a significant disadvantage of ASCII code that led to the development of Unicode. [2 marks]

....

....

....

....

....

For more help on this topic, see Letts GCSE Computer Science Revision Guide pages 44–45.

1   Sound, which is naturally analogue, is converted into a digital format through sampling. What is this process, and what impact does the sample rate have on file size?   [4 marks]

2   Define what 'bit depth' is and what impact it has on the quality of the sound.   [2 marks]

3   Two versions of the same tune, with the same sample rate, have very different file sizes. Explain why tune.wav is 50.4 MB and tune.mp3 is 3.43 MB.   [2 marks]

4   State what is meant by 'resolution' of a monitor. Explain what impact resolution has on the quality of graphics displayed.   [4 marks]

5   A JPEG file format uses lossy compression. Explain what this means for both the quality of the image and the size of the file.   [3 marks]

6   What is a 'pixel'?   [2 marks]

For more help on this topic, see Letts GCSE Computer Science Revision Guide pages 46–47.

1 Describe what a 'Huffman tree' is and what purpose it serves. [2 marks]

....

....

....

2 Describe what 'Run Length Encoding (RLE)' is. [2 marks]

....

....

....

3 Describe an example type of file where RLE is commonly used. [1 mark]

....

....

4 A Huffman tree for the text 2012 LONDON OLYMPICS is shown below.

Complete the missing sections. [5 marks]

For more help on this topic, see Letts GCSE Computer Science Revision Guide pages 48–49.

1 A client complains that their laptop computer is running very slowly, even though their anti-virus software is up to date.

Give **two** examples of how utility software could help free up some space on the hard drive. [2 marks]

....

....

2 On the motherboard, which element is used to connect different components in the CPU?

Tick **one** option. [1 mark]

Port ☐

Firewire ☐

Network ☐

Bus ☐

3 Define what 'hardware' is. [1 mark]

....

....

4 A client complains that their laptop is running very slowly, even though their anti-virus software is up to date, and they do not have a lot of data on their hard disk.

How could adding to the memory in the laptop help to solve this? [2 marks]

....

....

....

....

For more help on this topic, see Letts GCSE Computer Science Revision Guide pages 52–53.

5 Complete the following truth table for an OR logic gate. [2 marks]

A	B	A OR B
0	0	
0	1	
1	0	
1	1	

6 The image below is a black and white image of 25 pixels.

Explain why 25 bits would be needed to represent this image. [2 marks]

....

....

....

....

For more help on this topic, see Letts GCSE Computer Science Revision Guide pages 52–53.

1 System software and application software are two different types of software. Give **one** example of application software. [1 mark]

....

2 Which of the following is an example of a utility program?

Tick **one** option. [1 mark]

Spreadsheet ☐

Anti-virus checker ☐

Internet browser ☐

3 What is 'open source software'? [1 mark]

....

4 Explain the main difference between a Command Line Interface (CLI) and a Graphical User Interface (GUI). [4 marks]

....

....

....

....

5 Explain what the purpose of an operating system is. [5 marks]

....

....

....

....

....

6 Describe what a device driver does. [2 marks]

....

....

....

For more help on this topic, see Letts GCSE Computer Science Revision Guide pages 54–55.

1 What is the difference between volatile and non-volatile memory?

Give an example of each. [3 marks]

....

....

....

2 State what a 'Von Neumann bottleneck' is. [1 mark]

....

....

3 Describe briefly the 'fetch-execute cycle'. [1 mark]

....

....

4 Why are both RAM and ROM unsuitable alternatives to secondary storage? [2 marks]

....

....

5 Below are three different types of memory.

Tick the fastest from these types of memory. [1 mark]

Level 1 cache ☐

RAM ☐

Level 2 cache ☐

For more help on this topic, see Letts GCSE Computer Science Revision Guide pages 56–57.

Systems architecture

Module 22

6 When might a computer use virtual memory? [1 mark]

....

....

7 Describe why a computer uses cache memory. [2 marks]

....

....

8 What is a 'bus' on a motherboard? [1 mark]

....

9 In addition to the CPU clock speed, name **two** factors that can affect the CPU's performance. [2 marks]

....

....

....

....

For more help on this topic, see Letts GCSE Computer Science Revision Guide pages 56–57.

1 In addition to solid state and magnetic storage, name a type of secondary storage and give an example. [2 marks]

....

2 What is the difference between a '–R' and '–RW' in relation to an optional disc? [2 marks]

....

....

....

3 A small organisation wants to transfer all its data onto a cloud storage plan. Discuss the advantages and disadvantages of this option. [8 marks]

....

....

....

....

....

....

....

....

4 Explain, using an example, what is an 'embedded system' is. [2 marks]

....

....

....

....

5 Tablet computers and mobile phones tend to use solid state media for storage rather than hard drives. Describe **two** reasons, other than cost and capacity, why solid state is used. [4 marks]

....

....

Secondary storage

Module 23

For more help on this topic, see Letts GCSE Computer Science Revision Guide pages 58–59.

1 What is a 'Personal Area Network (PAN)'? [2 marks]

2 Explain the difference between a local area network (LAN) and a wide area network (WAN). Give an example of a situation where each might be used. [4 marks]

3 Which type of networking (wired or wireless) would you recommend for a small office with four people who use laptops and share a printer? Explain your answer. [5 marks]

4 "Schools should ban all onsite wireless connectivity for students."
Discuss this statement. [8 marks]

For more help on this topic, see Letts GCSE Computer Science Revision Guide pages 62–63.

1   Describe the differences between a star network topology and a mesh network
    topology.   [4 marks]

....

....

....

2   Draw an example of a ring network topology, showing clearly each of the components:
    printer, storage/server, three workstations.   [5 marks]

3   Describe how MAC address filtering supports security on a network.   [3 marks]

....

....

....

4   Identify the difference between whitelist and blacklist filtering. Explain which is the
    more secure. Explain which is more flexible.   [4 marks]

....

....

....

....

5   Why is a ring network vulnerable to system failure?   [2 marks]

....

....

Network topology

Module 25

For more help on this topic, see Letts GCSE Computer Science Revision Guide pages 64–65.

1 Draw a diagram identifying the basic four layers of the Internet.   [4 marks]

2 Describe the purpose of the 'Transport Layer' of the Internet.   [2 marks]

3 In online networks there are a number of protocols. What is a 'protocol'?   [2 marks]

4 Client-server communication:
   Tick **one** option in each case, showing whether the action would take place at the
   client end, server end or both.   [3 marks]

Action	CLIENT	SERVER	BOTH
Starting handshake			
Displaying HTML pages			
Receiving messages			

5 Describe what the 'client-server model' is.   [2 marks]

6 What elements may be found on the 'application layer' of the 4-layer Internet model?
   What purpose does the application layer serve?   [2 marks]

For more help on this topic, see Letts GCSE Computer Science Revision Guide pages 66–67.

1 In the context of cyber security, what is a 'Trojan horse'? [2 marks]

....

....

....

2 What is 'good password practice' in terms of security? Give **four** examples. [4 marks]

1. ....

2. ....

3. ....

4. ....

3 Explain why, when you forget your password, the company holding your account should send you a link to reset your password, not a copy of your password. [4 marks]

....

....

....

....

4 What is 'adware' and is it dangerous to your computer? [2 marks]

....

....

5 Describe **three** examples of phishing. [3 marks]

....

....

....

....

6 How is social engineering a threat to data security? [4 marks]

....

....

....

....

For more help on this topic, see Letts GCSE Computer Science Revision Guide pages 70–71.

7 How is 'malware' a threat to a network? [2 marks]

....

....

....

....

8 Why do networks have access levels for users?

Tick **one** option. [1 mark]

To give everyone access to download any files they want. ☐

To control the access different users have to information. ☐

To let the network manager know who is doing what on the network. ☐

9 What is Distributed Denial of Service (DDOS)? Describe what it does to a web server. [4 marks]

....

....

....

....

10 Describe how poor network policies can endanger the security of a network. [2 marks]

....

....

....

11 Why is it important to keep all software up to date, especially on a device that is attached to the Internet? [4 marks]

....

....

....

....

For more help on this topic, see Letts GCSE Computer Science Revision Guide pages 70–71.

1 Define the term 'encryption'. [2 marks]

....

....

2 What is the difference between encryption and encoding? Explain with examples. [4 marks]

....

....

....

....

3 Give **four** reasons why encryption is so important to online communication. [4 marks]

1. ....

2. ....

3. ....

4. ....

4 What does the 's' in https stand for? [1 mark]

....

5 What is a 'private key', and how does it support secure communication? [4 marks]

....

....

....

....

6 Modern organisations are spending increasing amounts of money on cyber security. This includes penetration testing, which is an attack by an organisation on its own computer system to identify weak points. What is the difference between black and white box penetration testing? [4 marks]

....

....

....

....

For more help on this topic, see Letts GCSE Computer Science Revision Guide pages 72–73.

Module 28

7   Identify **two** advantages and **two** disadvantages of a basic password system.   [4 marks]

....

....

....

....

8   What is the purpose of CAPTCHA elements on web forms?   [2 marks]

....

....

9   Name **two** potential disadvantages of CAPTCHA.   [2 marks]

....

....

....

10   **(a)** Define the term 'biometrics'.   [3 marks]

....

....

....

....

(b) Explain how biometrics can be a higher level of security than basic passwords.   [4 marks]

....

....

....

....

....

....

For more help on this topic, see Letts GCSE Computer Science Revision Guide pages 72–73.

1. The EU 'right to be forgotten' ruling allows individuals to request online data held about them to be erased. Many are concerned however that this may aid criminal activities. Whose rights should be prioritised? Give reasons for your answer. [6 marks]

2. Discuss whether the 'Internet of Things' is a good idea. [6 marks]

For more help on this topic, see Letts GCSE Computer Science Revision Guide pages 74–75.

Module 29

3 What are the security considerations for data storage in the 'cloud'?

Do you think these are outweighed by the convenience of this sort of storage?

Explain your answer. [6 marks]

....

....

....

....

....

....

4 Explain how a social network, based in the UK, must comply with the Data Protection Act. [6 marks]

....

....

....

....

....

....

For more help on this topic, see Letts GCSE Computer Science Revision Guide pages 74–75.

1 What is a simple 'Caesar cipher'? [1 mark]

2 Here is an example of a Caesar cipher:

A	B	C	D	E	F	G	H	I	J	K	L	M	N	O	P	Q	R	S	T	U	V	W	X	Y	Z
E	F	G	H	I	J	K	L	M	N	O	P	Q	R	S	T	U	V	W	X	Y	Z	A	B	C	D

Using the Caesar cipher above, decode this message. [1 mark]
CYOA YKILQPAN OYEJYA

3 How does hashing enhance the security of a sent message? [1 mark]

4 What is 'plaintext'? [1 mark]

5 Describe **two** reasons why encrypted data cannot be understood by an unauthorised person. [2 marks]

6 Identify **two** modern uses of online encryption. [2 marks]

1.

2.

7 A familiar method of encryption is SSL. Explain what SSL is and how it works. [4 marks]

For more help on this topic, see Letts GCSE Computer Science Revision Guide pages 76–77.

GCSE

Computer Science

Paper 1   Time: 1 hour 30 minutes

For this paper you must have:

- mathematical instruments

You must **not** use a calculator.

Instructions

- Use black ink or black ball-point pen. Use pencil only for drawing.
- Answer **all** the questions.
- Answer the questions in the spaces provided.
- Answer questions that require a coded solution in whichever format you prefer, as long as your meaning is clear and unambiguous.
- You must **not** use a calculator.

Information

- The mark for each question is shown in brackets.
- The maximum mark for this paper is 70.
- Remember to use good English and clear presentation in your answers.

Name: ....

1 State what 10010111 is translated from binary to decimal. **[1]**

2 State what 125 is translated from decimal to binary. **[1]**

3 Below are three types of memory. Tick the name of the type of memory used to make up for the difference of speed in function of two internal components of a computer. **[1]**

ROM ☐   cache ☐   volatile ☐

4 An early form of cipher is known as a Caesar cipher, as shown below:

A	B	C	D	E	F	G	H	I	J	K	L	M
N	O	P	Q	R	S	T	U	V	W	X	Y	Z

N	O	P	Q	R	S	T	U	V	W	X	Y	Z
A	B	C	D	E	F	G	H	I	J	K	L	M

a) Explain how the Caesar cipher works. **[2]**

b) Use the Caesar cipher above to decode the following: **[3]**

P	B	Z	C	H	G	R	E	F	.	H	F	R
O	V	A	N	E	L							

5 a) What is the 'client-server model'? **[1]**

b) Explain how it aids effective data transfer across the Internet. **[2]**

6 From the options below, identify (tick) **one** reason why hexadecimal is used to represent data. **[1]**

Hexadecimal is quicker for the computer to interpret. ☐

Hexadecimal takes up less memory in the computer. ☐

Hexadecimal is easier for humans to read. ☐

7 A list is made up of the following numbers:

58,34,2,4,39,54,1

Show the steps involved in sorting it using merge sort. **[2]**

....

....

....

....

8 The algorithm below is designed to search for a value within a list.

```
target <- 30
list <- [2,3,5,7,30,35]
found <- false
i <- 1
WHILE i≤6
    IF list[i] = target THEN
        found<- true
    ENDIF
    i = i + 1
ENDWHILE
```

a) Complete the trace table for this algorithm. The number of rows does **not** relate to the number of steps. **[4]**

target	found	i	list[i]
30	false	1	2

b) The algorithm is currently inefficient. One of the following lines should replace the WHILE statement above. Identify (tick) the correct replacement. **[1]**

WHILE found = false ☐

WHILE i<=6 OR found = false ☐

WHILE i<=6 OR found = true ☐

WHILE i<=6 AND found = false ☐

9 Below is the start of an algorithm to check when workers arrive and depart from their workplace. To make the output more user friendly, the programmer wants to make the program accept a 24-hour clock input and translate it into a 12-hour display. Complete the algorithm. **[4]**

```
OUTPUT<- "Enter the 24 hour number of arrival"
hour <-USERINPUT
```

10 A robot is controlled using an algorithm holding four subroutines:

FD (x) moves the robot x squares forward
LT (x) moves the robot x degree left
RT (x) moves the robot x degrees right
Obstacle() is a Boolean control registering TRUE if the way forward is blocked, FALSE otherwise.

a) Draw the path of the robot if it followed these instructions. **[2]**

```
FD (3)
LT (90)
FD (3)
RT (90)
FD (1)
```

START

b) Write the instructions so that the robot is able to follow this path. **[2]**

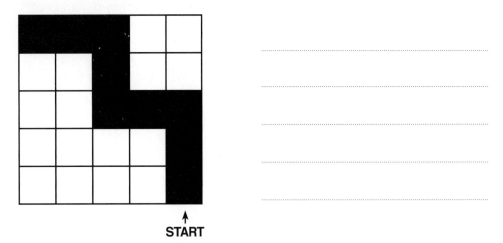

START

....

....

....

....

....

11 A Huffman tree for EVERYONE HAD FUN AT THE PARTY is shown below. Complete the missing elements in the table below. **[3]**

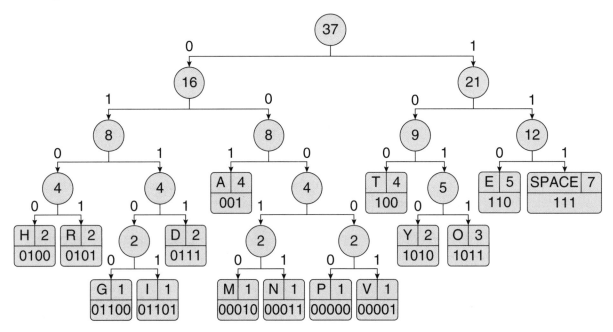

Character	Huffman coding
SPACE	
N	
A	

12 The two tables below form a relational database.

Stock:

StockName	Code	WarehouseLocation	Styles
T-shirt	TSH	Area45	2
Jeans	BJE	Area12	7
Trainers	TRA	Area09	1
Socks	SOX	Area25	1
Hoodie	SWH	Area40	4

Warehouse:

WarehouseLocation	SpaceUsed	Zone
Area45	15	A
Area12	30	B
Area09	30	C
Area25	8	C
Area40	15	A

a) State one field in the Warehouse table which will be the primary key. **[1]**

....

b) State how many records there are in the Stock table. **[1]**

....

c) Explain how the relationship between the two tables has been created. **[2]**

....

....

13 The black and white image below consists of 36 pixels.

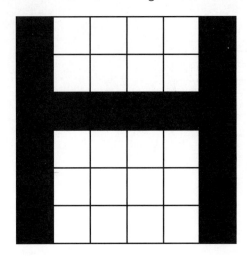

   a) Explain why 36 bits are required. [2]

   ....

   ....

   b) State how many bits would be needed if the image had four colours not two. [1]

   ....

14 Define the term 'resolution'. [1]

   ....

   ....

15 Explain the purpose of an operating system. [2]

   ....

   ....

16 In binary addition, show the result of 100101 + 10101. Show your working. [2]

   ....

   ....

17 Which of the following are common data types handled by most programming languages? Tick **two**. [2]

Maximum ☐

Character ☐

While ☐

Length ☐

Boolean ☐

18 Show the process in bubble sorting in the dataset below. [3]

16,21,11,19

....

....

....

....

....

....

19 In a bubble sort, tick the maximum number of swaps, if there are five numbers in the dataset to be sorted. [1]

2 ☐

10 ☐

25 ☐

30 ☐

20 What is the worst-case scenario for bubble sort? Explain why. [4]

....

....

....

....

....

21 Write an algorithm to calculate the average test score in a class of 10. You can use either pseudocode or a flowchart. **[4]**

22 State the index of the value 9 in the dataset below. For the purposes of this exercise, the index starts at [1]. **[1]**

23,12,4,9,1,30,3

23 Tick the following statements that are **true**. [1]

Arrays are of fixed size, so they cannot be edited without rewriting the code. ☐

Arrays allow only sequential access to the data they contain. ☐

Arrays can only store data of one type. ☐

24 The following code is a function:

```
FUNCTION HelloWorld (greeting,name)
   IF greeting[1] = "Hello"
      OUTPUT true
   ELSE
      OUTPUT false
   ENDIF
ENDFUNCTION
```

a) State the data structure for 'greeting'. [1]

....

b) State the data type for the output value. [1]

....

25 Give **two** reasons why programmers use functions. [2]

....

....

....

26 What is a 'parameter'? Tick **one**. [1]

A small section of a program ☐

A value used to control a function ☐

The data sent to a function by the subroutine that called it ☐

28 Tick the type of error that will allow the program to run, but will produce an incorrect answer. [1]

Run time error ☐

Logic error ☐

Syntax error ☐

28 Compare the benefits of coding in high-level and low-level programming language. Your answer should begin with a definition of each type of language. **[6]**

....

....

....

....

....

....

....

....

....

....

....

....

GCSE
Computer Science

Paper 2   Time: 1 hour 30 minutes

For this paper you must have:

- mathematical instruments

You must **not** use a calculator.

Instructions

- Use black ink or black ball-point pen. Use pencil only for drawing.
- Answer **all** the questions.
- Answer the questions in the spaces provided.
- Answer questions that require a coded solution in whichever format you prefer, as long as your meaning is clear and unambiguous.
- You must **not** use a calculator.

Information

- The mark for each question is shown in brackets.
- The maximum mark for this paper is 73.
- Remember to use good English and clear presentation in your answers.

Name: ....

1   Describe the differences between a **ring** network and a **bus** network, highlighting the
     advantages and disadvantages of each.   **[5 marks]**

....

....

....

....

....

....

2   Explain the difference between a LAN and a WAN. Give examples of both types of network.   **[4 marks]**

....

....

....

....

3   Discuss the following statement: **[6 marks]**

     "A wireless network is more convenient, but less secure, than a wired network."

....

....

....

....

....

....

4 Complete the following TCP/IP model of the Internet. **[3 marks]**

APPLICATION LAYER

_____ LAYER

_____ LAYER

_____ (or DATA LINK) LAYER

5 Below there are three network protocols. Tick **one** which is solely used by email communication. **[1 mark]**

TCP/IP ☐

IMAP ☐

HTML ☐

6 Communication across a network is expressed in Mbps. Calculate how many bits are being transmitted per second for a network with a 5 Mbps connection. **[3 marks]**

....

....

7 Complete the truth table for the following logic circuit: **[6 marks]**

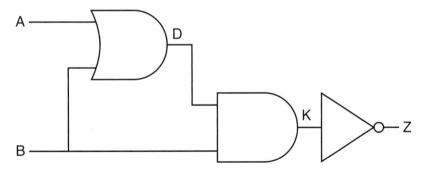

A	B	D	K	Z
0	0			
0	1			
1	0			
1	1			

8 Boolean operators are used in embedded systems.

a) State what an 'embedded system' is. **[1 mark]**

....

....

b) Describe **one** function of the embedded system in a washing machine. **[1 mark]**

....

....

9 Complete the truth table for the AND logic gate. **[1 mark]**

A	B	A AND B
0	0	
0	1	
1	0	
1	1	

10 A logic circuit is being developed for a lift door. The door has a sensor each side (A) and (B). The door opens when one is triggered, and can also be opened or closed using an override switch (O). The output is shown in Z. Complete the following logic circuit diagram. **[3 marks]**

A

B

Z

O

11 A small business wants to explore storing their data in the 'cloud'. One of their team is worried about this. Explain the benefits and potential disadvantages of storing data in the cloud. Your answer should include a clear definition of the 'cloud'. **[6 marks]**

....

....

....

....

....

....

12 Many people resist using files such as MP3 and JPG for their multimedia files.
Explain why this might be. **[2 marks]**

13 Tick the following statement that is **true** about run length encoding. **[1 mark]**

It is most effective on images with many continuous pixels of the same colour ☐

It is most effective on photographs ☐

It produces a lossy format ☐

14 One method of data compression is Huffman coding. Here are three types of data.
Tick the type that is compressed using Huffman coding. **[1 mark]**

Text data ☐

Graphical data ☐

Sound data ☐

15 Operating systems are an example of which type of software? Tick **one**. **[1 mark]**

Application software ☐

System software ☐

16 Describe what a 'high-level' programming language is. Explain why this is preferred by programmers
for some tasks. **[3 marks]**

17 "Subroutines make the process of algorithm writing easier". Discuss this statement. **[6 marks]**

18 A patch for an email application is available. Explain why users should always apply patches for software. **[2 marks]**

....

....

19 What is a data structure? Tick **one**. **[1 mark]**

A way of organising data so that it can be used efficiently ☐

A way of organising data so that it is neater ☐

A way of organising data so that it is easy to input ☐

20 Computer systems now manage critical data across our lives. Discuss **two** ways in which we can help ensure the safety and security of this data, whether at home, in school or at work. **[6 marks]**

....

....

....

....

....

....

....

....

....

....

21 a) State what 'data validation' is. **[1 mark]**

....

....

b) Identify **two** methods of validation. **[2 marks]**

....

....

....

....

22 The statements below are about variables. Tick the statement which is **true**. **[1 mark]**

A variable is data stored in memory that can be changed. ☐

A variable is data stored in memory that cannot be changed. ☐

A variable is created by the computer. ☐

23 A software entry screen requires a UK mobile phone number to be entered.
Describe the **three** types of test data that can be used and give examples of each. **[6 marks]**

ASCII table

Character	Decimal number	Binary number	Character	Decimal number	Binary number
blank space	32	0010 0000	^	94	0101 1110
!	33	0010 0001	-	95	0101 1111
"	34	0010 0010	'	96	0110 0000
#	35	0010 0011	a	97	0110 0001
$	36	0010 0100	b	98	0110 0010
A	65	0100 0001	c	99	0110 0011
B	66	0100 0010	d	100	0110 0100
C	67	0100 0011	e	101	0110 0101
D	68	0100 0100	f	102	0110 0110
E	69	0100 0101	g	103	0110 0111
F	70	0100 0110	h	104	0110 1000
G	71	0100 0111	i	105	0110 1001
H	72	0100 1000	j	106	0110 1010
I	73	0100 1001	k	107	0110 1011
J	74	0100 1010	l	108	0110 1100
K	75	0100 1011	m	109	0110 1101
L	76	0100 1100	n	110	0110 1110
M	77	0100 1101	o	111	0110 1111
N	78	0100 1110	p	112	0111 0000
O	79	0100 1111	q	113	0111 0001
P	80	0101 0000	r	114	0111 0010
Q	81	0101 0001	s	115	0111 0011
R	82	0101 0010	t	116	0111 0100
S	83	0101 0011	u	117	0111 0101
T	84	0101 0100	v	118	0111 0110
U	85	0101 0101	w	119	0111 0111
V	86	0101 0110	x	120	0111 1000
W	87	0101 0111	y	121	0111 1001
X	88	0101 1000	z	122	0111 1010

Answers

Module 1: Representing algorithms

1. An algorithm is a sequence of steps **(1)** that can be followed to complete a task **(1)**.
2. This flowchart outputs 'counting' **(1)**, then counts sequentially by 1s up to 5 **(1)** and outputs 'done' **(1)**.
3.

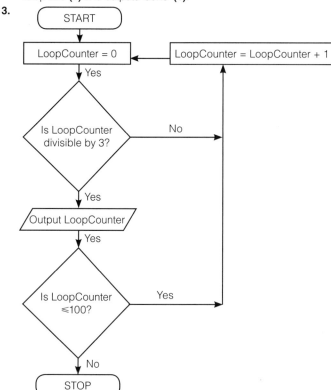

[5 marks: 1 mark for structure, 1 mark for each shape within the start/stop endings]

4. The amount of resources it uses in one complete cycle **(1)**. The time it takes to complete one complete cycle **(1)**.
5. Select Program
   Select File and Open
   Enter Password
   Edit Data
   Save and Close
   [5 marks: 1 mark for each entry correctly placed]
6. Iteration is repetition of a process **(1)**.
7. Breaking a problem into sub-problems **(1)**, each of which is a task on its own **(1)**.
8. Abstraction is the process of removing unnecessary details **(1)** from a problem or task such that a computer can process the task **(1)**.
9. A trace table works through the program line by line **(1)** to track the variables as they change through the program **(1)**.

Module 2: Searching algorithms

1. Calculate mid-point
   Compare value to mid-point
   If >, perform binary search on the left sub-list
   If <, perform binary search on the right sub-list **[4 marks: 1 mark for each step]**.
2. A linear search works by looking at every item or set of data in turn **(1)** until the details that you are searching for are found (or you fail to find it altogether) **(1)**.
3. Linear search **(1)** – you can see this because it goes from the first item in the array.
4. It is called brute force searching because it goes through each item without prioritising them, one by one, until it reaches the data sought **(1)**.

5. It starts its search at the middle value **(1)**, then splits the dataset **(1)** according to whether the data sought is above or below the middle value **(1)**.
6. If the data is unsorted **(1)** or the value is near the start of the file **(1)**.
7. Binary search **(1)** because the dataset is sorted **(1)**.
8. Linear search **(1)** because the list is fairly small and not sorted **(1)**.

Module 3: Sorting algorithms

1. A ✓ **(1)**
2. (6,2,4,1,8) to (2,6,4,1,8)
   (2,6,4,1,8) to (2,4,6,1,8)
   (2,4,6,1,8) to (2,4,1,6,8)
   (2,4,1,6,8) to (2,1,4,6,8)
   (2,1,4,6,8) to (1,2,4,6,8)
   Total five steps
   [4 marks: 1 mark for correct method, 2 marks for correct sequence, 1 mark for correct number of steps stated]
3.

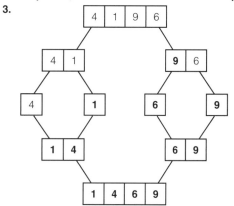

[3 marks: 1 mark for correct split, 1 mark for correct merge, 1 mark for correct answer]

Module 4: Data types

1. A Boolean data type has one of two values, generally identified as 'true' and 'false', or '1' and '0' **(1)**.
2. A telephone number would be a string **(1)** because it is used as an identifier **(1)** and is not used as a basis for any calculations **(1)**.
3. In computer science a variable is a location in memory **(1)** used to store data, it has an identifier **(1)**. The value within this location can change as a result of the processes operated by the program **(1)**.
4. 5 **(1)**
5. When you declare a constant you also give it a value at the point of declaration **(1)**; constants cannot be modified or assigned a new value without rewriting the code **(1)**. An example would be DaysInYear = 365. When you declare a variable, you are uniquely identifying **(1)** a space in memory that will hold a value **(1)** that can be manipulated by code. An example would be HoursWorked = input("Hours worked this week: ")
6. Iteration **(1)**: also known as repeating a set of instructions a number of times.
7. Iteration allows the programmer to code one sequence of steps to be run through a set number of times **(1)** to achieve a required outcome, without having to write that set of steps repeatedly **(1)**. This keeps code shorter **(1)** and makes it easier to test **(1)**. You may not know how many times code has to run, so cannot physically write it.

Module 5: Pseudocode

1. Pseudocode is an informal set of programming language style instructions for an algorithm or program **(1)** that is designed to be easily read and doesn't use any specific syntax **(1)**.

2.
```
Input student mark
If student mark > 30
    print 'passed'
Else (1)
    print 'did not pass'
End (1)
```
3. Counts **(1)** and prints **(1)** numbers up to 100 **(1)**.
4. Prints all numbers between a user-set start and finish point **(1)**, printing an error message **(1)** if the start number is larger than the finish number **(1)**.
5.
```
Input Number1
Input Number2
Input Number3 (1)
Sum = Number1+Number2+Number3
print "The sum of the numbers is: " + "Sum (1)
Product = Number1*Number2*Number3"
print "The product of the numbers is: " + "Product" (1)
```

Module 6: Arithmetic, relational and Boolean operators in programming languages

1.
```
Input a
input b
c = a*b
print c (1)
```
2. Code 1 would show the integer value of 13/2, which is 7 **(1)**. Code 2 would show the 'real' or 'float' value, which is 6.5 **(1)**. The integer value is the rounded up whole number result of the calculation **(1)**.
3. Because you cannot use mathematical operators on strings like 'Name': you can only use mathematical operators on numbers **(1)**.
4. The coder used division (/) on the calculation of pay based on hours worked and pay rate **(1)**. This should have been a * for multiplication **(1)**.
5. Although b has a value lower than 50, a is greater than 10 **(1)**, so the printout would be 'Extra Homework!" **(1)**.
6. b still has the lower value, but now the code is looking for a being equal to or greater than 10 **(1)**. So now the display shows "Class Dismissed!" **(1)**.

Module 7: Flowcharts

1. a = decision **(1)**
   b = terminator (START/STOP) **(1)**
   c = input/output **(1)**
   d = process **(1)**
2. When an input value is entered, the flowchart checks if it is greater than or equal to 10 **(1)**. If it is not, the "Outside acceptable range" statement is given and resets **(1)**. If it is, the flowchart checks if it is also equal to or less than 20 **(1)**. If not, it resets again and if it is, the final "Acceptable range" message is given and the flowchart stops **(1)**.
3.

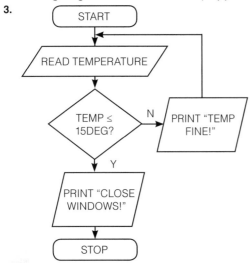

(2)

Module 8: Data structures

1.

1	1	1	1
1	0	0	0
1	0	0	0
1	1	1	1

(2)

2. Data structures define how data is formatted and stored **(1)** to allow for efficient search, retrieval and processing **(1)**.
3. Output would be "pears" **(1)** because all lists are indexed starting at 0 **(1)**.
4. No **(1)** because arrays do not accept mixed data types **(1)**.
5. The array has 6x6 elements **(1)** – 36 in total **(1)**.
6. 6 is the 5th item **(1)** because all indexes start at 0.
7. An array is static in that its size is fixed and cannot be updated **(1)**.

Module 9: Input/output and file handling

1. It would open a csv file **(1)** called contacts **(1)**. It then asks the user to input their name and phone number **(1)** and then saves the new data to the file **(1)**.
2. External sensors **(1)**, e.g. temperature, movement or sound. User input **(1)**, e.g. keyboard, mouse, touchscreen.
3. An index allows the computer to search the database more effectively **(1)**, because it is possible to search the index **(1)** rather than the whole database to locate the element sought.
4. Because the computer cannot check if you are telling the truth **(1)** – only that the data you enter is within the limits that have been set **(1)**.
5.
```
file = open("classlist.csv", "a")
name (1) = input("Please enter name.")
file.write (1) (name + ","+ "\n")
```
6. The file would be overwritten everyday, meaning older versions could not be accessed **(1)**. A solution would be to create a daily backup with an alternative filename **(1)**.

Module 10: String handling

1. A string data type can contain any alphanumeric character **(1)**, including punctuation **(1)**.
2.

Data type	Store as an integer	Store as a string
Steve		✓
15	✓	
007		✓
2010	✓	
10.2		✓
01501 2987659		✓

[4 marks if fully correct, 3 marks if four correct, 2 marks if three correct, 1 mark if one correct]

3. "fishchipsmushy peas" **(1)** because there is no clear space set up between the strings **(1)**.
4. 102 **(1)**
5. So that the computer can distinguish between the two possible data entries, as in passwords, for example **(1)**.

Module 11: Random number generation in a programming language

1. A random number is generated by a process with an outcome that cannot be predicted or reproduced **(1)**. A pseudorandom number is a computer-generated random number that appears to have the same properties but is created using statistical patterns that can be repeated and therefore it is not truly random **(1)**.

Answers

2. Any two from: user ID generation; online gambling; computer games; online password generators; cryptography services.
[2 marks: 1 mark for each use]
3. It chooses a random integer **(1)** of value between 1 and 100 **(1)**, and encourages the users to guess the number. It counts the number of guesses and outputs that number as part of the message **(1)** when the user gets the number right. The random function in this code ensures that truly no one knows in advance the value of the number to be guessed **(1)**.

Module 12: Databases
1. A flat-file database has only one table **(1)**, such as an Excel worksheet which shows the prices of products in a store **(1)**. A relational database has several different tables linked together **(1)**, such as a school database that contains details of students, staff, classes **(1)**.
2. A primary key is a data entry uniquely identified to each record within the database **(1)**.
3. Structured data is data organised into a specific format **(1)**, such as your contacts on your phone **(1)**. Unstructured data is like a list of your IMs or the contents of your social media photo account **(1)**: there is no coherent organisation **(1)**.
4. To output the data in a way that is easy for humans to read **(1)**.
5. (a)

| D | 335948 | Shirt | White | M | £12.99 | **(1)** |

(b)

| D | 335948 | Shirt | White | M | £12.99 |
| F | 222687 | Shirt | Blue | M | £12.99 |

[2 marks: 1 mark for each correct row]

(c)

A	569875	T-shirt	Blue	S	£14.99
D	335948	Shirt	White	M	£12.99
E	798994	Socks	White	5	£6.99
F	222687	Shirt	Blue	M	£12.99

[4 marks: 1 mark for each correct row]

Module 13: Introduction to subroutines and structured programming
1. Any three from: clearly breaking a big task into little ones makes the big task more achievable; using self-contained code modules or subroutines (one for each part of the task) makes it easy to see which part of the code does which part of the overall task; updates are a lot easier – you just change the bit that needs to be updated; can be called from the main program, or another subroutine.
[3 marks: 1 mark for each correct example]
2. A comment is an annotation of the code only relevant to the human reader – the computer overlooks it. It helps the human reader see what is supposed to happen, and is identified using a convention **(1)** such as #Total The Amount in this section **(1)**.
3. Assembler **(1)**: A program that translates assembly language into machine code **(1)**.
Compiler **(1)**: A program that translates high-level programmer written code into low-level machine code **(1)**.
Interpreter **(1)**: A program that translates programmer code line by line **(1)** into machine code.
4. 1. Comments in the code **(1)**
   2. Clear variable names **(1)**
   3. Modules and functions appropriately named **(1)**
   4. Use indented code where available **(1)**

Module 14: Parameters and subroutines
1. Any one from: name; value **(1)**.
2. Any two from: the code can be written once, then used more than once, as needed, such as a greenhouse temperature monitoring system; keeps code shorter because you are only writing the code once for the subroutine, no matter how many times you need it, your code overall can be considerably shorter; easier to test even large tasks, if decomposed into smaller subtasks, can be easy to test one module – or subroutine – at a time; you can access and use any variable from your main code without having to redefine it.
[2 marks: 1 mark for each example]
3. Accept an answer such as:
```
Sub ImageCheck (1)
maxFileSize = 1 (1)
input "file to be uploaded" (1)
Check file properties (1)
IF filesize <= max
      UPLOAD file
ELSE
      output "file too large" (1)
ENDIF
EndSub (1)
```
4. (a)

START **(1)**

(b)

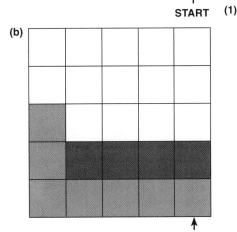

START **(1)**

(c) Accept answers such as:
FD (1)
LT (90)
FD (3)
RT (90)
FD (4)
RT (90)
FD (3) **(1)**

Module 15: Robust and secure programming

1. Validation ensures that the data is within reasonable limits **(1)**, such as a date of birth, or a postcode **(1)**. It does not test whether the data is actually true **(1)**.
   Verification checks whether the data is true **(1)**, and this is generally a human task **(1)** rather than a computer one. Date of birth, for example, can be confirmed with a birth certificate or driver's licence or passport **(1)**.
2. Accept answers such as:
   Make some answers 'required' so that they can rank against them.
   Ask for the same information in different ways so that if the answers differ then something isn't right.
   [2 marks: 1 mark for method, 1 mark for description]
3. Accept answers such as:
   TimeIn >= 0700 AND TimeIn < 1200. 'nine o'clock' would be invalid.
   [2 marks if fully correct, 1 mark for valid time control]
4. Any two from: making sure the program runs without errors; testing confirms that the product that has been created to meet the original specification criteria or problem; mimicking user input with different data to make sure all possible values are dealt with appropriately; eliminating the need to withdraw and re-release a program.
   [2 marks: 1 mark for each point made]
5. Normal: e.g. 01/10/1974 **(1)**
   Extreme: 01/01/2000 or 31/12/1999 **(1)**
   Erroneous: e.g. 5th June 1969 **(1)**

Module 16: Number bases and binary arithmetic

1. It is easier to translate into decimal **(1)**, easier to understand **(1)**. Each hexadecimal digit represents 4 bits, or a nibble, so two hexadecimal digits represent a byte **(1)**.
2. A = 10 * 16, 2 = 2
   160 + 2 = 162   **[2 marks: 1 mark for correct working, 1 mark for correct answer]**
3.   00000111
     + 00000111
       00001110
   [2 marks: 1 mark for correct working, 1 mark for correct answer]
4. 16^2 16^1 16^0
   = 256   16   1
   ≈ 1   0   0
   = 100
   [2 marks: 1 mark for correct working, 1 mark for correct answer]

Module 17: Units of information and character encoding

1. **(a)** 8 **(1)**
   (b) 256 **(1)**
   (c) 2048 **(1)**
2. Any one from: 1 coded as black and 0 as white; 1 as white and 0 as black **(1)**.
3. A nibble **(1)**
4. A gigabyte (GB) is 1024 megabytes **(1)**.
   A terabyte (TB) is 1024 gigabytes **(1)**.
5. There are 16 possible binary numbers **(1)**, so 16 possible codes may be actioned **(1)**.
6. 256 colours **(1)**
7. Colour depth is used to describe the maximum number of colours that could be used in the graphic **(1)**. The higher the number of colours then the more complex the colour palette – and the larger the file size **(1)**.
8. The original 128 characters within ASCII are not sufficient to represent all of the possible characters, numbers and symbols in languages across the world **(1)**. Unicode includes the non-Western languages that ASCII doesn't recognise or accommodate **(1)**. Unicode has separate character sets for the majority of written languages across the globe.

Module 18: Representing images and sound

1. The program takes a number of samples of the sound at regular set intervals **(1)**, and works out the 'top' and 'bottom' values of the analogue sound within each sample **(1)**. If the sound being processed is 'above' the halfway point, the program checks again if the sound would still be above halfway if the first half was cut into half again, and so on. 'Above' is recorded as a '1', 'below' it is recorded as a '0' **(1)**. The more samples per second that are taken, the higher the quality of sound – and the larger the file **(1)**.
2. Bit depth is the number of bits available for each sample taken from the sound **(1)**. The greater the bit depth, the better the quality of sound **(1)**.
3. MP3 is a lossy compression format so a lot of data is lost in the compression, thus reducing the size.
   or
   WAV is a lossless compression format so very little data is lost in compression, meaning that the file size isn't reduced as substantially.
   [2 marks: 1 mark for description, 1 mark for explanation]
4. Resolution refers to how many pixels are used per square **(1)**. Low-resolution graphics are coarser **(1)** and may seem 'furry'; high resolution graphics have more pixels per square **(1)** and therefore are clearer and sharper **(1)**.
5. JPEGs allow compression of graphics in a lossy format, meaning that data quality is lost **(1)** as the file is increasingly compressed **(1)**, but JPEGs can also be saved in full uncompressed detail **(1)**.
6. A pixel is short for Picture Element, and is a single 'dot' on your screen or printout **(1)**. It is a square of one colour used to make a bitmap image **(1)**.

Module 19: Data compression

1. A Huffman tree shows the frequency of elements in a file, coding the most frequent ones with the smallest number **(1)**, to limit the file size overall in a lossless compression strategy **(1)**.
2. RLE is a very simple form of lossless data compression **(1)** which converts consecutive identical elements by storing the number of identical elements as a code **(1)**.
3. When it is used on images that have many continuous identical colour pixels black and white image, for example **(1)**.
4.

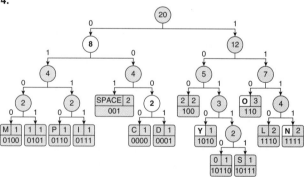

[5 marks: 1 mark for each correct element]

Module 20: Hardware, software and Boolean logic

1. Any two from: defragmentation software moves file blocks closer together; so that the computer can load files more quickly; compression software reduces file sizes using less space so that the files may be loaded more quickly; some type of backup software could be used to move files to a secure place, then the user could delete the less often used

Answers

files on the hard disc to free up space; which would improve the speed of the disc. **[2 marks: 1 mark for each correct example]**
2. Bus ✓ **(1)**
3. Hardware is the collective name given to the physical (or electrical) components (or parts) of a computer system **(1)**.
4. RAM memory is the workspace of the computer. If there isn't enough capacity in memory for the CPU needs, the computer has to set up what's known as a virtual memory file **(1)**. To do this the CPU reserves space on the hard disk to simulate (or pretend to be) additional RAM. This process, referred to as 'swapping', slows the system down **(1)**.
5.

A	B	A OR B
0	0	**0**
0	1	**1**
1	0	**1**
1	1	**1**

[2 marks if fully correct, 1 mark for the first two lines]
6. Two colours are needed so only two possible bit patterns – which can be represented with one bit showing either 0 or 1 **(1)**: therefore 25 pixels will need 25 bits **(1)**.

Module 21: Software classification
1. Any one from: word processing; spreadsheet; desktop publishing **(1)**. It is not enough to simply name a product like 'Keynote' or 'Word'.
2. Anti-virus checker ✓ **(1)**
3. Open source software is provided with a licence that means it can be downloaded, along with its source code, used, edited or redistributed for any purpose **(1)**.
4. A Command Line Interface is the text based way of communicating with the computer **(1)**. It is not particularly efficient nor is it user friendly **(1)**. A Graphical User Interface is the basis of most systems today, like iOS, WindowsX and MacOSx, where icons replace the words **(1)** and a mouse is used more than a keyboard **(1)**.
5. The OS is needed to provide an interface between application software/user and hardware **(1)** and to handle input/output devices **(1)**. It is responsible for memory management **(1)** and for allocating processor time **(1)**. It also provides security **(1)**.
6. A device driver is a small program or software interface **(1)** that enables an operating system to communicate with a hardware device **(1)** such as a printer or graphics card.

Module 22: Systems architecture
1. Volatile memory (such as Read Access Memory) **(1)** will only hold data in memory as long as there is a power source, whereas non-volatile memory (such as USB storage) **(1)** will keep contents when power is disconnected **(1)**.
2. A Von Neumann bottleneck occurs when an 'instruction fetch' and 'data operation' cannot occur at the same time because they use the same bus **(1)**.
3. The fetch-execute cycle is the process by which the CPU reads (fetches) instructions from the memory cache, decodes them, and then operates – or executes – the instruction **(1)**.
4. RAM loses its content when the power is switched off **(1)** and ROM is read-only so cannot be edited **(1)**.
5. Level 1 cache ✓ **(1)**
6. Virtual memory is a section of the hard drive that is used when the computer does not have access to enough RAM to complete the tasks in the program **(1)**.
7. The computer uses cache memory as a form of buffer because the CPU works faster than RAM **(1)**. The data is pushed into cache memory before the CPU needs it to stop the slower memory inhibiting the function of the CPU **(1)**.
8. Buses are wires around the motherboard that connect the components that are attached **(1)**.
9. The number of cores **(1)** and the cache memory **(1)**.

Module 23: Secondary storage
1. Optical **(1)**. CD/DVD/Blu-ray **(1)**
2. A '–R' disc can only be written to once **(1)** whereas a '–RW' disc can be erased and re-written multiple times **(1)**.
3. You can come to either conclusion – that cloud storage is a good or not-so-good option for the organisation. Your comments should include elements such as:

Advantages of cloud storage	Disadvantages of cloud storage
Access from anywhere with Internet connection. So if they have travelling representatives they can access files and update diaries, for example.	You need a reliable Internet connection – especially if you are handling large files. So if they have travelling representatives they might be trying to access diaries or online files and find that they cannot.
For businesses, this means that offices across the world can access the same files.	You are relying on someone else to keep your files safe.
Disaster recovery is easier – assuming that your storage provider wasn't affected by whatever hit your system. So if the organisation is holding staff and customer data it is easier to recover without imposing on the people.	Moving from one provider to another can be difficult. So you need to be sure that they meet the standards you need as a small organisation.
Costs are generally lower per MB and storage capacity is more flexible than local storage. So this can be a better idea for a small organisation that is balancing costs carefully.	There can be data ownership issues if your provider is sold to another company – when Facebook bought Instagram, all Instagram content transferred a 'licence to use' that content to Facebook – without users' express consent. So the data they hold might well be given away to a bigger company, breaking the law. They need to be sure that this is not going to happen.

[8 marks: 0–2 marks – A poor response containing little explanation of advantages and disadvantages. No use of technical language and poor use of spelling and grammar; 3–5 marks – A response is given that relates to the scenario. Some advantages and disadvantages are given with some explanation. Some examples are provided and there is some use of technical language. Only minor errors in spelling and grammar; 6–8 marks – A detailed response is given that is related to the scenario. Advantages and disadvantages are given and explained fully. There is a balanced discussion and all examples are relevant and appropriate. There are few, if any, errors in spelling and grammar.]
4. An embedded system is one in which the computer system plays a part in a much bigger device. The computer element is often nearly invisible, but essential **(1)**. Examples include digital watches/MP3 players/traffic lights **(1)**.

5. Any two from: solid state media can be more compact than magnetic media: the smaller size enables better portability; the battery will last longer because solid state media uses less power; speed of access is higher in solid state drives so you can more quickly access your data; solid state is silent, so it can be used in a wider variety of settings.
[4 marks: 2 marks for each reason]

Module 24: Definitions and types of networks

1. A network often based on Bluetooth connection between devices such as keyboards, pointing devices, phones, audio headsets and printers **(1)**. These cover very short distances (up to about 10 metres) but have the advantage that they can move with the user **(1)**.

2. A LAN is a network in which all connected devices are relatively close together, in a single building or premises **(1)** like a school or office complex **(1)**. A WAN is a network in which the connected devices are too thinly spread to make a physical connection **(1)** and is used by multinational organisations and even the Internet could be described as a WAN **(1)**.

3. Wireless **(1)**. Suitable if they use their laptops in a portable manner (e.g. hot desking) **(1)**, if they all work in a relatively small area and can rely on appropriate WAP points **(1)**, if their network connection is secure (i.e. password protected) **(1)** and if there isn't a lot of heavy traffic (e.g. video streaming) across the network **(1)**.

4. You can argue for either point of view, just make sure you include evidence such as:
Allowing wireless connectivity means:
- it allows students to make use of their own portable devices in their learning;
- maintaining a safe learning environment is very important as students are more vulnerable to safety issues (like trailing wires);
- it allows computing devices to be used outside of the lesson, e.g. in PE or drama;
- schools have limited budgets and it is cheaper to add extra wireless devices to a school network;
- less cable and drilling are needed when expanding the network and this may save money;
- there are now many devices which don't have wired connection ports and schools/students may want to be able to use these devices.

And barring wireless connectivity means:
- wired networks can provide high bandwidth for when students make use of a lot of multimedia;
- schools need high bandwidth / reliable systems as delays in lessons are not acceptable;
- there is better security on wired networks, making it easier for schools to control/monitor how students are using the network;
- network performance may be poor if there are large numbers of student-owned devices using the school network at any one time.

[8 marks: 0–2 marks – A poor response containing little justification for the argument. No use of technical language and poor use of spelling and grammar; 3–5 marks – A response is given that relates to the scenario. Some justification for the argument. Some examples are provided and there is some use of technical language. Only minor errors in spelling and grammar; 6–8 marks – A detailed response is given that is related to the scenario. Detailed justification for the argument. There is a balanced discussion and all examples are relevant and appropriate. There are few, if any, errors in spelling and grammar.]

Module 25: Network topology

1. A star network topology has one connection to each of the resources or devices on it **(1)**, while a mesh network connects every device to every other device **(1)**. While the mesh network is more robust **(1)**, it is also a lot more expensive. **(1)**

2. Example answer:

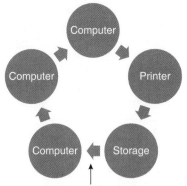

Network cable between each component

[5 marks: 1 mark per element. Must include network cable and clear indication of the comms between devices and the ID of the devices]

3. Each device has its own MAC address **(1)**. If the firewall has a list of those authorised to use the network resources, the MAC address of a new device can be checked against that whitelist **(1)**: if it isn't there the network is sealed against that device **(1)**.

4. A whitelist identifies authorised sites if on an Internet filter, or users or machines if on a firewall. Only those on the whitelist are allowed through. A blacklist bars only those devices or addresses identified on the list **(1)**. A whitelist is more secure **(1)**, but a blacklist is more flexible **(1)**, since the whitelist provides an absolute and limited list of devices or sites which are allowed, while the blacklist just blocks the resources or sites identified **(1)**.

5. Each packet of data has to travel through all of the devices between its origin and its destination **(1)**. If one device malfunctions the whole network is compromised **(1)**.

Module 26: Communication protocols

1.

APPLICATION LAYER
TRANSPORT LAYER
INTERNET LAYER
NETWORK ACCESS (or DATA LINK) LAYER

[4 marks: 1 mark for each layer]

2. The Transport Layer sets up the communication between the sender and the destination, making sure they agree the 'language' and also that the recipient knows the size and number of packets that it should expect **(1)**. If any go astray the Transport Layer automatically tries a number of times to re-send before transmitting a 'failed' message to the original sender so that they know the message went astray **(1)**.

3. Protocols are a set of communication standards **(1)** that govern transfer of data between devices **(1)**.

4.

Action	CLIENT	SERVER	BOTH
Starting handshake	✓		
Displaying HTML pages	✓		
Receiving messages			✓

[3 marks: 1 mark for each tick]

5. This model spreads the workload between the main server and the user's device **(1)**: a client device may share resources with the more powerful server, which enables faster communication because the server does the work before transmission **(1)**.

6. The application layer is the top-most layer and it includes protocols like DNS, HTTP(s), SMTP, IMAP, SSH, FTP **(1)**. This controls how applications access data and communicate **(1)**.

Module 27: Definition, purpose and threat

1. A Trojan horse is a malicious computer program **(1)** that appears to the user to be of legitimate use but actually causes damage to the computer it is installed on **(1)**.

2. Accept answers such as:
Uses a range of characters, ideally including punctuation.
More than 8 characters long.
Not based on a word.
Not based on any easily known personal information (pet name, post code…).
Easily remembered so not written down.
Regularly (and frequently) changed.
Not used more than once.
[4 marks: 1 mark for each example]

3. Emails can be intercepted **(1)** so should never include sensitive material **(1)**. It might not be you asking for the password information **(1)**, so this might be unauthorised access **(1)**.

4. Adware is advertisements which are included in the software program and are displayed at intervals during use **(1)**. Could be dangerous, you don't know what is included, or who has built it, and it may include cookies and/or spyware **(1)**.

5. Any three from: fraudulently obtaining information by claiming to be a reputable organisation; pretending to be a bank and requesting login details; emailing a user to update personal details via a false website; creating false versions of existing websites. **[3 marks: 1 mark for each point made]**

6. Social engineering attempts to trick a user into revealing their password **(1)** and other security information through ruses such as pretending to be a new employee, or a colleague from another branch, or someone begging you for help **(1)**. Humans generally want to trust other humans, and since most of the time the request is genuine this is a hard one to beat. Asking to contact them back on an organisation phone extension can be one method of defence **(1)**, since email addresses can easily be faked **(1)**.

7. Malware can deliberately encrypt data, delete or corrupt data, destroy hard drives **(1)**, and generally cause considerable harm and distress **(1)**.

8. To control the access different users have to information ✓ **(1)**

9. This is when a site is attacked by a number of systems causing the server to shut down access to legitimate users or even entirely shut down **(1)**. A strategy for the attacker is to compromise one computer and take over its access to the Internet, then use it to infect others with malware that allows them to be controlled also **(1)**. A computer under the control of an attacker is known as a 'zombie' or 'bot' **(1)**, and botnets (collections of these hijacked computers) are often considered one of the biggest current threats to Internet security **(1)**.

10. Allowing accounts to remain of people who have left the organisation, or allowing anyone to self-register, means that the network is open to any type of abuse **(1)** – witting or unwitting. No one who does not have the right to access should have that access. No one should have more access to network resources than they absolutely need **(1)**.

11. Browser and operating system, driver and application software, are regularly updated **(1)** to ensure robustness and security **(1)** – and malware writers are constantly benefitting from those who delay their updating **(1)**. A loophole/error/back entrance may have been found that puts the computer at risk **(1)**.

Module 28: Detecting and preventing threats

1. Encryption is the process of changing information or data **(1)** into a form that may only be understood by a recipient who has the key to decrypt it **(1)**.

2. Encoding is a way of changing information into data that the computer can process **(1)** such as changing 'Male or Female' into 'M or F' **(1)**.
Encryption on the other hand makes the message impossible to understand by anyone who does not have the key **(1)** such as the enigma machine in WWII **(1)**.

3. 1. Online communication of personal data has to be encrypted to be safe.
2. Governments use online secure data to transmit messages to outlying offices and embassies.
3. Online commerce needs customers to be able to securely transmit payment details.
4. Online banking requires that account holders can access their accounts safely.
[4 marks: 1 mark for each reason]

4. Secure **(1)**

5. A private key is a very small code **(1)** used by anyone to encrypt messages **(1)** intended for a particular recipient, ensuring that the encrypted messages can be decrypted only by using a second key **(1)** that is known only to the recipient **(1)**.

6. While a 'white box' penetration test simulates an attack **(1)** by a malicious insider who knows something of the computer system under attack **(1)**, a 'black box' test simulates external hacking **(1)** or cyber warfare **(1)**.

7. Advantages – any two from: cheapest security system of all; if frequently changed, passwords can be among the most secure access devices; no specialist hardware required.
Disadvantages – any two from: people forget them; vulnerable to brute force attacks and keyloggers; depend on users using a secure combination – and only once for each login. **[4 marks: 2 marks for two advantages, 2 marks for two disadvantages]**

8. CAPTCHA is supposed to identify human access to the site **(1)** as opposed to automated computer access **(1)**.

9. Any two from: can be difficult to read – especially for people with visual impairments; some browsers don't render them accurately ; not popular with users; audio version isn't always clear enough to understand; requires a keyboard so not entirely user friendly.
[2 marks: 1 mark for each disadvantage]

10. (a) This is a term used in computer security to refer to the use of physical characteristics **(1)** which are unique to each person as a password or security element **(1)**, such as fingerprints or retinal scans **(1)**.
(b) Passwords are often forgotten **(1)**.
Passwords are often easily hacked **(1)**.
Biometrics are unique to each person **(1)**.
You can't forget a biometric – it's your finger or eye scan **(1)**.

Module 29: Ethics

1. Answers to include:
   - Definition of the right to be forgotten – that individuals have the right – under certain conditions – to ask.
   - Search engines to remove links with personal information about them.
   - Current news about people who have been reported as using this right (such as Mario Costeja Gonzalez, who provided the test case).
   - Clearly supported reasoning behind opinion, e.g.
     - Innocent people shouldn't have to drag around incorrect online stories
     - The Internet doesn't forget
     - Internet searches help check on prospective employees or partners

   [6 marks: 0–2 marks – A poor response containing little justification for the argument. No use of technical language and poor use of spelling and grammar; 3–4 marks – A response is given that relates to the scenario. Some justification for the argument. Some examples are provided and there is some use of technical language. Only minor errors in spelling and grammar; 5–6 marks – A detailed response is given that is related to the scenario. Detailed justification for the argument. There is a balanced discussion and all examples are relevant and appropriate. There are few, if any, errors in spelling and grammar.]

2. Define Internet of Things: the network of physical objects or 'things' embedded with electronics, software, sensors, and connectivity to the Internet.
   Argument (positive or negative) including evidence such as:
   - A smart home helps people who are disabled live a more 'normal' or mainstream life.
   - When computers monitor presence in a home and can be hacked – is this a privacy concern?
   - If your fridge can keep a watch and report to your doctor on how much chocolate you eat – does this erode your individual rights to eat what you choose?
   - If your phone can check your heart rate if you are at risk of a heart attack, or it can check if you're about to suffer an epileptic fit – doesn't that reassure you and your family?

   [6 marks: 0–2 marks – A poor response containing little justification for the argument. No use of technical language and poor use of spelling and grammar; 3–4 marks – A response is given that relates to the scenario. Some justification for the argument. Some examples are provided and there is some use of technical language. Only minor errors in spelling and grammar; 5–6 marks – A detailed response is given that is related to the scenario. Detailed justification for the argument. There is a balanced discussion and all examples are relevant and appropriate. There are few, if any, errors in spelling and grammar.]

3. Answers to include elements such as:
   - The owner of the servers might be bought out or go bankrupt: what happens to your data?
   - The servers might be hacked.
   - The legal framework might change of the country where the data is stored – e.g. 'safe harbor' rules of the US and the 2015 EU decision to not accept this.
   - Online storage allows data files to be accessed from anywhere with online access.
   - Online storage allows collaboration between colleagues on one file.

   [6 marks: 0–2 marks – A poor response containing little justification for the argument. No use of technical language and poor use of spelling and grammar; 3–4 marks – A response is given that relates to the scenario. Some justification for the argument. Some examples are provided and there is some use of technical language. Only minor errors in spelling and grammar; 5–6 marks – A detailed response is given that is related to the scenario. Detailed justification for the argument. There is a balanced discussion and all examples are relevant and appropriate. There are few, if any, errors in spelling and grammar.]

4. Answers to include elements such as:
   - Data should be fairly and lawfully processed.
   - Data should only be used or disclosed for the specified notified purposes.
   - Data should be adequate, relevant and not excessive.
   - Data should be accurate and kept up to date.
   - Data should not be kept any longer than necessary.
   - Access must be provided for individuals to check and correct their data, with a right of explanation when a computer takes automated decisions based on the data.
   - Data should not be transferred outside the European Union except to countries with adequate data protection legislation.

   [6 marks: 0–2 marks – A poor response containing little justification for the argument. No use of technical language and poor use of spelling and grammar; 3–4 marks – A response is given that relates to the scenario. Some justification for the argument. Some examples are provided and there is some use of technical language. Only minor errors in spelling and grammar; 5–6 marks – A detailed response is given that is related to the scenario. Detailed justification for the argument. There is a balanced discussion and all examples are relevant and appropriate. There are few, if any, errors in spelling and grammar.]

Module 30: Encryption

1. This is a simple 'shift' cipher, whereby each letter represents another in a logical sequence **(1)**.
2. GCSE COMPUTER SCIENCE **(1)**
3. Hashing is used to check whether anyone has tried to break the code before sending it on. Any changes to anything in the content will produce a garbled or changed message when the legitimate key is used **(1)**.
4. Plaintext is an unencrypted message **(1)**.
5. Encrypted data is deliberately scrambled so that it cannot be understood straight off **(1)**. The unauthorised person would not have the key to decrypt the data **(1)**.
6. Answers to include:
   E-commerce
   Online banking
   Secure messaging
   Government business
   [2 marks: 1 mark for each use identified]
7. SSL stands for 'secure sockets layer', a protocol that uses a key to encrypt data **(1)** across the Internet using two keys: a public key accessible to all and a private key known only to the recipient of the message **(1)**. This combination is the only way in which secure communication is possible **(1)**. Your browser connects to the website and requests an identity check from the server, to make sure that the server sends a recognised SSL certificate. If this is part of a list the browser holds, then all is well. If not, the browser will ask the user 'Are you sure you want to deal with the owners of this website? I don't know them!' At this point it is a good idea to pause and check you have typed the correct URL, because this is a hint that something isn't necessarily right. If the certificate is recognised, the URL changes from HTTP to HTTPS and you can continue your session in an encrypted mode **(1)**.

Paper 1

1. 151 **(1)**
2. 1111101 **(1)**
3. cache ✓ **(1)**
4. **a)** A Caesar cipher is a set of alphabetical letters set against a second set, but 'shifted' a set number of places so that each letter is paired against a different one in the opposing set **(1)**. When a message is encoded, the coded letters (not the original message) are sent to the recipient, who can decode the message only if they know the 'shift' **(1)**.

   b)

P	B	Z	C	H	G	R	E	F		H	F	R
C	O	M	P	U	T	E	R	S		U	S	E
O	V	A	N	E	L							
B	I	N	A	R	Y							

   [3 marks: 1 mark for each correct word decoded]

5. **a)** A client-server model spreads the workload between the main server and the user's device **(1)**.

   b) A client device may share resources with the more powerful server **(1)**, which enables faster communication because the server does the work before transmission **(1)**.

6. Hexadecimal is easier for humans to read ✓ **(1)**
7. 58,34,2,4,39,54,1 = starting
   34, 58   2,4   54,39   1
       2,4   34,58   39,54,1
   1,2,4,34,39,54,58 = finishing

   [2 marks: 1 mark for correct steps, 1 mark for correct outcome]

8. **a)**

target	found	i	list[i]
30	false	1	2
		2	3
		3	5
		4	7
		5	30
	true	6	35

   [4 marks: 1 mark for each correct column]

   b) `WHILE i<=6 AND found = false` ✓ **(1)**

9. Example answer:
```
IF hour = 0 THEN
     OUTPUT 12
     OUTPUT 'am'
ELSE    IF hour < 12 THEN
     OUTPUT hour
     OUTPUT 'am'
ELSE        IF hour = 12 THEN
     OUTPUT 12
     OUTPUT 'pm'
ELSE            hour ← hour - 12
                OUTPUT hour
                OUTPUT 'pm'
                ENDIF
     ENDIF
ENDIF
```
(4)

10. **a)**

    FD (3)
    LT (90)
    FD (3)
    RT (90)
    FD (1)

    START   **(2)**

    b) FD (3)
    LT (90)
    FD (2)
    RT (90)
    FD (2)
    LT (90)
    FD (2) **(2)**

11.
Character	Huffman coding
SPACE	111
N	00011
A	001

    [3 marks: 1 mark for each correct row]

12. **a)** WarehouseLocation **(1)**

    b) 5 **(1)**

    c) The primary key **(1)** from Warehouse is a field in the Stock table **(1)**.

13. **a)** Each bit can hold two colours **(1)** – 36 pixels in a two-colour image need 36 bits **(1)**.

    b) 2 per pixel **(1)**

14. Resolution is the number of pixels per set size, e.g. per inch, not in the overall image **(1)**.

15. An operating system manages the computer resources and is the interface between the user and the computer **(1)**. It controls memory and processing time, manages access rights of users and handles errors **(1)**.

16. 100101
    + 10101
    111010

    [2 marks: 1 mark for correct working and 1 mark for correct answer]

17. Character ✓ **(1)**
    Boolean ✓ **(1)**

18. 16,21,11,19 -> 16,11,19,21 -> 11,16,19,21 **[3 marks: 1 mark for each stage. Mark for last stage will only be awarded when the other stages are correct]**

19. 10 ✓ **(1)**

20. The worst situation for bubble sort is when the list is effectively in reversed order, so that every element **(1)** is in the 'wrong' position **(1)** and must be moved on each pass so that the sort will need to make the maximum number of passes **(1)** through the list.

21. Example answers:
```
Set total to zero
Set score counter to one
While score counter is less than or equal to ten
     Input the next score
     Add the score into the total
Set the class average to the total divided by ten
Print the class average.
```

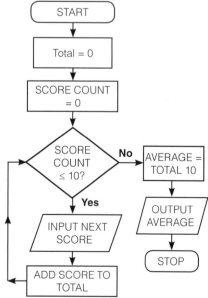

[4 marks: 1 mark for right sequence, 1 mark for loop, 1 mark for accurate calculation, 1 mark for output]

22. Position (or index) 4 **(1)**
23. Arrays are of fixed size, so they cannot be edited without rewriting the code. ✓
    Arrays can only store data of one type. ✓ **[1 mark: both correct for 1 mark]**
24. Array **(1)**
    Boolean **(1)**
25. Any two from: to make code easier to read; to allow for code reuse/sharing; to improve code maintenance/make the code easier to update; to reduce programmer error. **[2 marks: 1 mark for each answer]**
26. The data sent to a function by the subroutine that called it ✓ **(1)**
27. Logic error ✓ **(1)**
28. Answers to include:
    High-level languages are human readable, but must be compiled or interpreted to be processed by the computer. Low-level languages are closer to machine code, but are hard for humans to read.
    If you write in a low-level language you have much more control over the performance of the code and processor, while in a high-level language you are dependent on the compiler. If you write in a high-level language you can more easily debug an error track it, since it is easier for humans to read.
    Low-level languages take longer to write and check than high-level languages, but writing code in high-level languages loses some of the time benefit because the code must be compiled.
    Low-level languages are harder for humans to learn than high-level languages.
    [6 marks: 1–2 marks: There are a few simple or vague statements relating to the question. The form and style of writing has many deficiencies. Ideas are not often clearly expressed. Sentences and paragraphs are often not well-connected or at times bullet points may have been used. Specialist vocabulary has been used inappropriately or not at all. Much of the text is legible and some of the meaning is clear. There are many errors of spelling, punctuation and grammar but it should still be possible to understand much of the response. 3–4 marks: There is evidence of some evaluation shown through the use of mostly correct technical explanation linked with advantages in the situation given. The answer covers a few of the ideas above or includes other correct answers. The form and style of writing is appropriate to the purpose and some complex ideas are expressed reasonably clearly and fluently. Well linked sentences and paragraphs are usually used. Specialist vocabulary has been used on a number of occasions but not always appropriately. Text is legible and most of the meaning is clear. There are occasional errors of spelling, punctuation and grammar. 5–6 marks: There is evidence of a clear evaluation shown by a correct explanation and three well justified comments. The answer covers most of the ideas above or includes other correct answers. The form and style of writing is appropriate to the purpose and complex ideas are expressed clearly and fluently. Sentences and paragraphs follow on from one another clearly and coherently. Specialist vocabulary has been used appropriately throughout. Text is legible and the meaning is clear. There are few, if any, errors of spelling, punctuation and grammar.]

Paper 2
1. Answers to include:
   A bus network has a central spine of network cabling (called a bus) while a ring network has all of the computers connected to each other in a circle.
   A bus network is simple and cheapest to install and is good for a temporary network. It is flexible because elements can be removed or added without messing with the rest of the network. It is best used in small or temporary networks and can be a useful home network solution. A ring network can offer fast data flow when it is working well – all data flows in one direction. Even when the load is the same, this performs better than a bus setup. Each device can access the resources on the network equally.
   Both have disadvantages, however. In a bus network, if the bus (spine) fails the whole network crashes. Performance is affected by load so the more devices attached, the slower it functions. Bus cables are limited in length, so the network is limited in size, and must be terminated properly to avoid reflection of signal, which can crash the system. Data has to 'queue' sometimes because the bus is busy with other demands. In a ring network, each packet of data has to travel through all of the devices between its origin and its destination. If one device malfunctions the whole network is compromised. Setting this up is more expensive than a bus network. **[5 marks: 1 mark for each correct point made]**
2. A LAN is a network in which all connected devices are relatively close together **(1)**, in a single building or premises, like a school or office complex **(1)**. A WAN, on the other hand, is a network in which the connected devices are too thinly spread to make a physical connection **(1)**. These tend to be connected through telephone lines, undersea cables and, in extreme cases, satellite links **(1)**.
3. Answers to include:
   A wired network offers a more reliable connection because the link is physical. This means that it is also usually faster than wireless connections. It is less convenient because it ties the device to one place, but because the data is transferred through a physical link it is more secure.
   A wireless network allows more freedom of movement, although you can lose signal under less than ideal conditions. Sharing a wireless access point with other users can also slow the speed of any data transfer. Security can be an issue since data is broadcast rather than contained within a cable.
   [6 marks: 1–2 marks: There are a few simple or vague statements relating to the question. The form and style of writing has many deficiencies. Ideas are not often clearly expressed. Sentences and paragraphs are often not well-connected or at times bullet points may have been used. Specialist vocabulary has been used inappropriately or not at all. Much of the text is legible and some of the meaning is clear. There are many errors of spelling, punctuation and grammar but it should still be possible to understand much of the response. 3–4 marks: There is evidence of some evaluation shown through the use of mostly correct technical explanation linked with advantages in the situation given. The answer covers a few of the ideas above or includes other correct answers. The form and style of writing is appropriate to the purpose and some complex ideas are expressed reasonably clearly and fluently. Well linked sentences and paragraphs are usually used. Specialist vocabulary has been used on a number of occasions but not always appropriately.

Text is legible and most of the meaning is clear. There are occasional errors of spelling, punctuation and grammar. 5–6 marks: There is evidence of a clear evaluation shown by a correct explanation and three well justified comments. The answer covers most of the ideas above or includes other correct answers. The form and style of writing is appropriate to the purpose and complex ideas are expressed clearly and fluently. Sentences and paragraphs follow on from one another clearly and coherently. Specialist vocabulary has been used appropriately throughout. Text is legible and the meaning is clear. There are few, if any, errors of spelling, punctuation and grammar.]

4.

APPLICATION LAYER

TRANSPORT LAYER

INTERNET LAYER

NETWORK ACCESS (or DATA LINK) LAYER

[3 marks: 1 mark for each correct layer]

5. IMAP ✓ **(1)**
6. 5 megabits per second = 5 000 000 bits per second **(3)**
7.

A	B	D	K	Z
0	0	0	0	1
0	1	1	1	0
1	0	1	0	1
1	1	1	1	0

[6 marks: 2 marks for each correct column]

8. **a)** An embedded system is part of a larger system, such as traffic lights, and is designed to work without human intervention. Usually the 'computer' part is invisible to the user **(1)**.

    b) Any one from: senses cloth quality and density to identify quantity of water needed; detect water temperature; manage wash cycle **(1)**.

9.

A	B	A AND B
0	0	0
0	1	0
1	0	0
1	1	1

(1)

10.

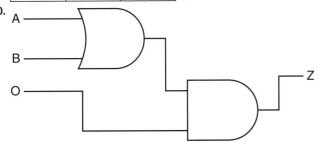

[3 marks: 1 mark for A and B into an OR gate, 1 mark for O and the output of A and B into an AND gate, 1 mark for the output of the gate with O as an input with its output connected to Z]

11. Cloud storage is the term for storing your data on computer systems belonging to someone else, and accessing them through the Internet **(1)**. Advantages of cloud storage include that you may access them from anywhere with an Internet connection **(1)**, and can therefore collaborate with people regardless of distance or time. Local disaster recovery is easier too, since you can restore from an online backup **(1)**. Costs are generally lower per MB than local storage **(1)**. On the other hand, however, your data is stored on someone else's computer, so you need to be sure of their security measures **(1)**, and of ownership of your data should that company be bought or go into bankruptcy. Moving what can be considerable amounts of data from one provider to another can also cause problems **(1)**.

12. Both file types use compression to reduce file size **(1)** and therefore people may be concerned about the loss of quality as both remove either image elements or certain audio frequencies **(1)**.

13. It is most effective on images with many continuous pixels of the same colour ✓ **(1)**

14. Text data ✓ **(1)**

15. System software ✓ **(1)**

16. Instructions are close to English/easier for humans to read and write than a low-level language, which means a programmer is less likely to make errors **(1)**. It's quicker to develop code and easier to maintain high level code **(1)**. High-level languages are usually available across many platforms or chipsets or operating systems **(1)**.

17. You can come to either stance but you need to use evidence to support your response. Answers to include:
The advantages of using subroutines over writing the code repeatedly as needed include clearly breaking a big task into little ones makes the big task more achievable. Using code modules or subroutines (one for each part of the task) makes it easy to see which part of the code does which part of the overall task. Updates are a lot easier – you just change the bit that needs to be updated. A subroutine may work perfectly one time that it is called, but the main code may then change the variable used by the subroutine – and the subroutine may fail. Finally, testing through the entire code checking, each iteration of each subroutine, can feel like an endless task. **[6 marks: 1 mark for each point made]**

18. A patch will fix any known security issues **(1)** so the machine running the application is less vulnerable to cyberattack **(1)**.

19. A way of organising data so that it can be used efficiently ✓ **(1)**

20. Answers to include: Backup (ideally off-site) to help make sure that if data is corrupted in some way the copy may be used; Passwords to ensure only authorised people gain access to the data; Access levels to help ensure that only the right people gain access to editing or creation options; Redundancy – keeping a parallel system (or resources) running ready to take over if anything happens to the main system (or resources).

[6 marks: 1–2 marks: There are a few simple or vague statements relating to the question. The form and style of writing used has many deficiencies. Ideas are not often clearly expressed. Sentences and paragraphs are often not well-connected or at times bullet points may have been used. Specialist vocabulary has been used inappropriately or not at all. Much of the text is legible and some of the meaning is clear. There are many errors of spelling, punctuation and grammar but it should still be possible to understand much of the response. 3–4 marks: There is evidence of some evaluation shown through the use of mostly correct technical explanation linked with advantages in the situation given. The answer covers a few of the ideas above or includes other correct answers. The form and

style of writing used is appropriate to purpose and expresses some complex ideas reasonably clearly and fluently. Well linked sentences and paragraphs are usually used. Specialist vocabulary has been used on a number of occasions but not always appropriately. Text is legible and most of the meaning is clear. There are occasional errors of spelling, punctuation and grammar. 5–6 marks: There is evidence of a clear evaluation shown by a correct explanation and three well justified comments. The answer covers most of the ideas above or includes other correct answers. A form and style of writing appropriate to purpose is used and complex ideas are expressed clearly and fluently. Sentences and paragraphs follow on from one another clearly and coherently. Specialist vocabulary has been used appropriately throughout. Text is legible and the meaning is clear. There are few if any errors of spelling, punctuation and grammar.]

21. **a)** Validation is an automatic computer check to ensure that the data entered is sensible and reasonable **(1)**.

    b) Any two from: check digit; format check; length check; lookup limit; presence check; range check

    [2 marks: 1 mark for each correct answer]

22. A variable is data stored in memory that can be changed. ✓

23. Normal (or typical) **(1)**: e.g. 07625738925 **(1)**
    Extreme (or boundary) **(1)**: 07000000000 or 07999999999 **(1)**
    Erroneous **(1)**: e.g. Sheffield71155 **(1)**

Notes

Notes